Roman Gloucestershire

Cirencester with Ermin Street running north-west towards Gloucester

Roman Gloucestershire

Alan McWhirr
Leicester Polytechnic

ALAN SUTTON &
GLOUCESTERSHIRE COUNTY LIBRARY
1986

Alan Sutton Publishing Limited
17a Brunswick Road
Gloucester

First published 1981
Reprinted 1986

British Library Cataloguing in Publication Data

McWhirr, Alan
    Roman Gloucestershire.
    1. Gloucestershire — History
    I. Title
    936.2'2'41   DA670.G4

    ISBN 0—904387—60—7

Acknowledgement is given to the Ermin
Street Guard for their co-operation
in the cover photograph.

Typesetting and origination by
Alan Sutton Publishing Limited.
Photoset Stempel Garamond 10/12
Printed in Great Britain

Contents

TO
Helen, Rachel and James

Preface

The modern county of Gloucestershire boasts two important Roman cities and a remarkable collection of villas, along with a host of other settlements associated with agriculture and industry. The Fosse Way runs the length of the county and significant stretches of other roads, such as Ermin Street and Akeman Street, pass through. The recent publication by the Royal Commission on Historical Monuments of their *Inventory of Iron Age and Romano-British Monuments in the Gloucestershire Cotswolds* has brought before the archaeological world a wealth of material upon which to draw. It includes details of some recent excavations such as those at Barnsley, Frocester and Kingscote, but has appeared too early to include the remarkable excavations at Uley, and does not deal with Cirencester or Gloucester. This book attempts to bring together what is known about the whole of Roman Gloucestershire, but, with the absence of detailed published accounts of the Forest or Vale, the Cotswolds still dominate what follows. It is aimed at the interested layman, and although some of the illustrations which are included have already appeared in print and will be well known to archaeologists, the opportunity has been taken to bring together as many as possible in one book.

The enthusiastic work of many individuals, both on a full- and part-time basis, means that as research in the county progresses Gloucestershire will continue to feature regularly in the pages of archaeological literature both at home and abroad.

Alan McWhirr,
Leicester Polytechnic
November 1980

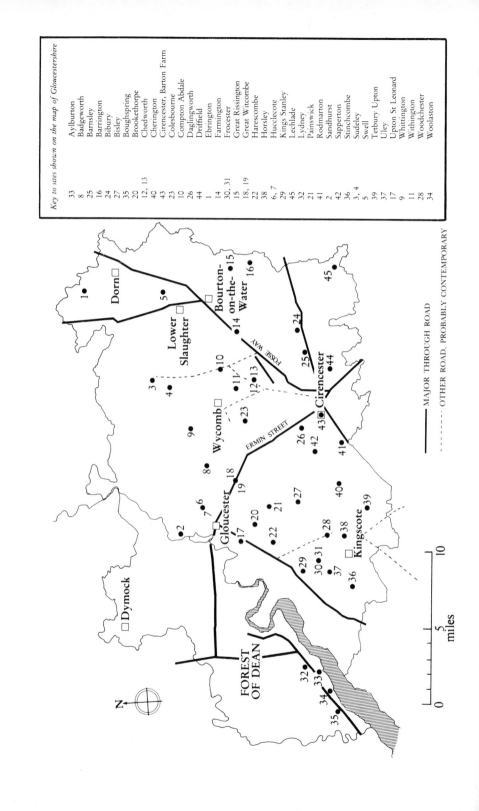

1
The Arrival of the Romans

In 55 and 54 B.C. Julius Caesar led two expeditions to Britain, probably with the intention of capturing the island on the second occasion. However, a series of revolts in Gaul late in 54 B.C. and again in 53 B.C. diverted Caesar's attention and, unable to return, he abandoned the attempt to bring Britain into the Roman world. Some time later, Caesar wrote an account of his campaigns in Gaul and Britain which provides a valuable insight into the nature of the inhabitants and also helps us to understand the way in which these people lived during the first century B.C. For example, Caesar describes how the British engaged the enemy in battle:-

In chariot fighting the Britons begin by driving all over the field hurling javelins, and generally the terror inspired by the horses and the noise of the wheels are sufficient to throw their opponents' ranks into disorder. Then, after making their way between the squadrons of their own cavalry, they jump down from the chariots and engage on foot . . . They combine the mobility of cavalry with the staying-power of infantry.

However he does not restrict himself to purely military activities, but describes the country and its people:-

The interior of Britain is inhabited by people who claim, on the strength of oral tradition, to be aboriginal; the coast, by Belgic immigrants who came to plunder and make war — nearly all of them retaining the names of the tribes from which they originated — and later settled down to till the soil. The population is exceedingly large, the ground thickly studded with homesteads, closely resembling those of the Gauls, and the cattle very numerous.
For money they use either bronze, or gold coins, or iron ingots of fixed weight. Tin is found inland, and small quantities of iron near the coast; copper that they use is imported. There is timber of every kind, as in Gaul, except beech and fir. Hares, fowl and geese they think it unlawful to eat, but rear them for pleasure and amusement. The climate is more temperate than in Gaul, the cold being less severe. The island is triangular, with one side facing Gaul . . .

As with all historical accounts one has to be aware of the possibility of inaccuracies and bias, but even so, considered along with the archaeological evidence, Caesar's account enables a picture of life in lowland Britain two thousand years ago to be compiled.

At the time of the Roman conquest, some ninety years after Caesar's expeditions, lowland Britain was organised into tribal groups, each with its own hierarchical structure. Caesar actually mentions the names of some tribes and their leaders, and we know of others from different writings and from coins, which during the late first century B.C. and in the first century A.D. were often inscribed. As can be seen by the way in which these various tribes reacted towards Caesar and later Claudius, they were independent of each other, although at times some united against a common foe, whether from across the sea or at home.

In the late Iron Age the area covered by the present county of Gloucestershire was in the tribal kingdom of the *Dobunni*. The extent of their tribal

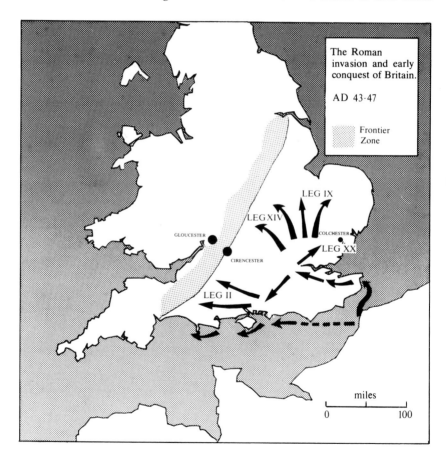

The Roman invasion and early conquest of Britain.

AD 43-47

Frontier Zone

lands and the names of their kings can be deduced by a study of the coins they minted, and these suggest that, at the time of the conquest in A.D.43, the territory was divided into two. Excavations and fieldwork at Bagendon 4.8km north of Cirencester indicate the site of a possible capital for the tribe, as coin moulds used for producing coins have been found which are unlikely to have been made anywhere else other than in the official mint in the chief settlement of the tribe. King Boduocus was probably living at Bagendon, or *Corinion* as it might have been called. The western part of the tribal lands were at some time apparently governed separately by a king whose name is not fully known but begins Corio . . . He may have been based at Minchinhampton where extensive earthworks indicate a site of some importance.

Despite tribal rivalry, Britain was stable enough to engage in trade and is recorded as exporting corn, cattle, hides and hounds along with gold, silver and iron. The economy of the country was based on the land and the bulk of the population lived and worked on farms. When the Roman army eventually occupied the country they were keen to foster this thriving agricultural system, and so, once the pockets of anti-Roman feeling were dealt with, local people were encouraged to work with and for the Roman administration.

Such, briefly, was the state of Britain when the Roman army, comprising legionary and auxiliary soldiers, landed on the shores of Kent in the summer of A.D.43 and proceeded to march on Colchester, crossing the Rivers Medway and Thames on route. It was commanded by Aulus Plautius and contained four legions, the IInd *Augusta*, IXth *Hispana*, XIVth *Gemina* and the XXth *Valeria* and an approximately equal number of auxiliary troops. In all the expeditionary force was made up of some 40-50,000 men. Wishing to gain the maximum political advantage from this victory, Claudius had given instructions that the army should await his arrival before entering Colchester, intending to lead the victorious troops himself accompanied by elephants, a sight which must have caused awe and amazement amongst the native population. Whilst in Britain, Claudius probably received the formal surrender of a number of tribes, as the inscription on the Arch of Claudius commemorating the triumph indicates. One of these may well have been the *Dobunni*.

Within three to four years the Roman army had occupied most of the country south and east of a line from the River Severn to the River Humber, and had established a frontier zone linking the two rivers and extending beyond to the south-west. A road, later to become known as the Fosse Way, was constructed in the frontier zone to facilitate the rapid deployment of troops and the movement of supplies. Its name in Roman times is unknown. Forts were built in the military zone, some on the Fosse Way, others in front and some behind. In Gloucestershire there are three places where structural evidence of a military installation has been found: at Cirencester,

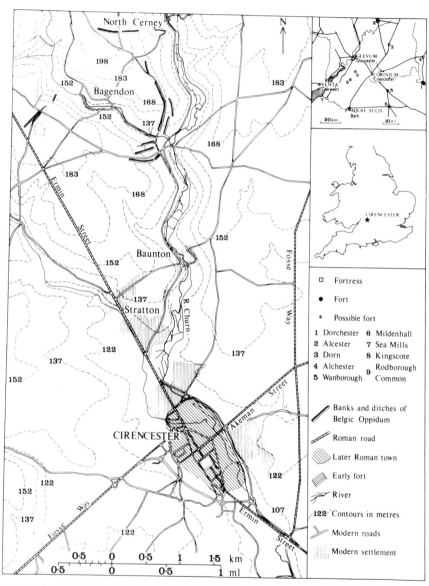

Map to show the relationship of Cirencester and Bagendon.

Kingsholm and Gloucester. Other Roman sites have produced objects or features in the ground which may have been military in origin, but as yet cannot be proved to have been forts or fortresses.

CIRENCESTER

The discovery in the nineteenth century of two tombstones recording auxiliary soldiers has long indicated that a detachment of the Roman army was based at Cirencester, but it was not until 1961 that the site of a fort was positively identified by excavation. The tombstones were found in the Watermoor area of Cirencester close to Ermin Street, which linked Silchester with Cirencester and eventually Gloucester, and they each record cavalry-men from different regiments. One was erected to Sextus Valerius Genialis who was forty years old and had served in the army for twenty years, having originally come from the low countries. The expanded inscription reads:

> SEXTVS·VALE
> RIVS·GENIALIS
> EQES·ALAE TRHAEC
> CIVIS FRISIAVS TVR
> GENIALIS AN XXXX STXX
> H S E E F C

which translated means:

> Sextus Valerius Genialis
> trooper of the Cavalry Regiment of
> Thracians, a tribesman of the Frisii,
> from the troop of Genialis, aged 40,
> of 20 years' service, lies buried here.
> His heir had this set up.

Above the inscription is a carving showing the deceased as a mounted trooper riding down a fallen enemy. On his left arm he carries a hexagonal shield and a standard, and in his right hand he wields his lance. The stone stands 2.1m high and is made of the local oolitic limestone. Sextus Valerius Genialis was a member of the *ala Thracum*, a cavalry unit of 500 men, which probably was included with the invasion force accompanying the XXth legion. If Genialis had joined the unit only just before it arrived in Britain, and as he died after 20 years' service, then the tombstone must have been erected before A.D.63. His unit could well have been moved into the region from Colchester after the foundation of the *colonia* there in c. A.D.50.

A second tombstone commemorates Dannicus, the dedication to whom reads:-

> DANNICVS EQES ALAE
> INDIAN TVR ALBANI

Tombstone of Sextus Valerius Genialis found at Cirencester.

STIP XVI CIVES RAVR
CVR FVLVIVS NATALIS IT
FL. .IVSBITVCVS EX TESTAME
    H   S   E

which translated reads:

> Dannicus, trooper of the Cavalry Regiment Indiana,
> from the troop of Albanus, of 16 year's service,
> a tribesman of the Raurici, lies buried here.
> Fulvius Natalis and Flavius Bitucus had this
> erected under his will.

The carving at the top of the tombstone shows the deceased as a mounted trooper riding down a fallen enemy whom he is about to strike with his lance. Dannicus was a tribesman of the *Raurici*, whose chief town was the Roman colony of *Augusta Raurici*, the modern Augst, near Basel in Switzerland. He was a member of a cavalry regiment of 500 men, the *Ala Indiana*. The most recent ideas about the date of this tombstone depend upon the name of his heir *Flavius Bitucus*, who presumably lived after A.D.70 as he was named after the emperor *Flavius Vespasianus*. However, the reading here is difficult and it may not be Flavius.

So the evidence that we have in the form of inscriptions indicates that two different cavalry regiments were based at Cirencester. This agrees with the evidence from metalwork, found by chance and from excavations, which has all been shown to be from the uniform and equipment of auxiliary soldiers. The first indication of the fort in which these troops lived came from the 1961 excavations in the grounds of Leaholme just to the south of The Avenue. Here Mr John Wacher found a rampart and associated ditches of military character in several places. These features, along with observations in 1964 in Chester Street, have led to a tentative plan of the fort being put forward. The area within the defences is about 1.8 hectares which was just about big enough for a cavalry unit of 500 men. Whether the same fort was used by the different detachments of auxiliary troops indicated by the inscriptions cannot be determined, but it is most likely that it was. Excavations in fact suggest that the internal layout was reorganised in three stages, which might reflect three different units rather than the two indicated by the tombstones.

Two other sections of bank or rampart have been found in Cirencester which have a military appearance. One was found when the later town defences were excavated in the grounds of the former Watermoor Hospital (now the headquarters of the Cotswold District Council). It consisted of a gravel bank with turf cheeks, and in the rear face an oven had been constructed, a feature often noted in forts. The other section of military rampart came to light during excavations in Watermoor at the corner of

Tombstone of Dannicus found at Cirencester.

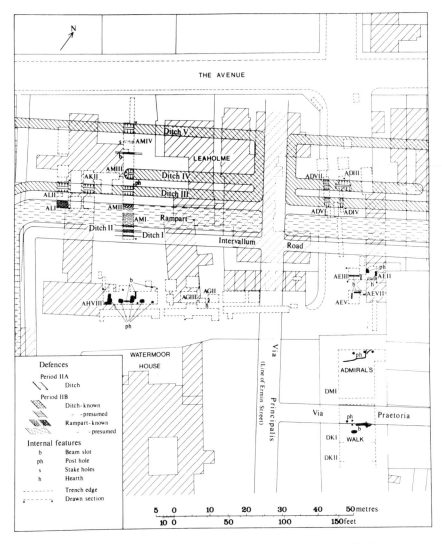

Details of the fort found during excavations at Leaholme and Admiral's Walk, Cirencester.

Chesterton Lane and Watermoor Road on a small plot of land then known as The Sands. Here a 12m length of rampart was traced and shown to consist of a gravel bank with turf cheeks back and front, all resting on a rammed gravel base. The profile of the ditch was unlike those usually found around forts of the Roman army, but this may be due to the high level of the water table making it unnecessary and impracticable to dig the usual V-shaped ditch with cleaning channel along the bottom. There is, however, the slight

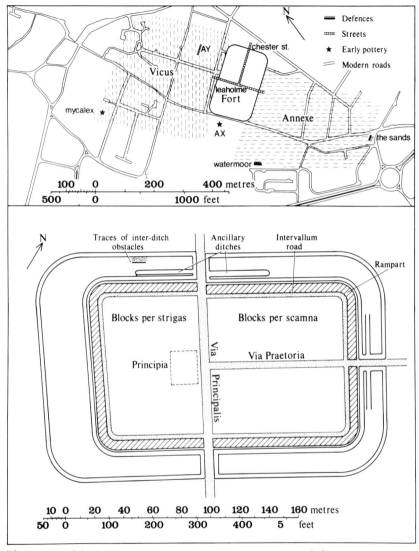

The position of the fort at Cirencester and a possible reconstructioned plan.

possibility that this rampart and ditch belonged to a later phase than the military occupation. If the ramparts found at Watermoor Hospital and The Sands were military then they would appear to have belonged to annexes to the fort further north. It is surely significant that the military cemetery from which the inscribed tombstones came respected the line of The Sands rampart.

The fill from the fort ditch contained pottery of a type which suggests, along with other datable material found from within the fort, that military occupation lasted until the late 70s, possibly into the decade A.D.75-85, and that the army had, therefore, been based in Cirencester for about thirty years. The size of the unit, a cavalry regiment of 500 men, suggests that activity was one of policing a wide area, presumably including the previous strongpoint of the *Dobunni* at Bagendon north of Cirencester. When the legions were pulled out of the area, the auxiliary troops went with them and Cirencester was vacated, leaving behind a thriving trading community which for thirty years had profited from the presence of the army.

KINGSHOLM
Excavations in the district of Kingsholm in 1972 confirmed the long-held view that a fort or fortress once existed there on the banks of the old course

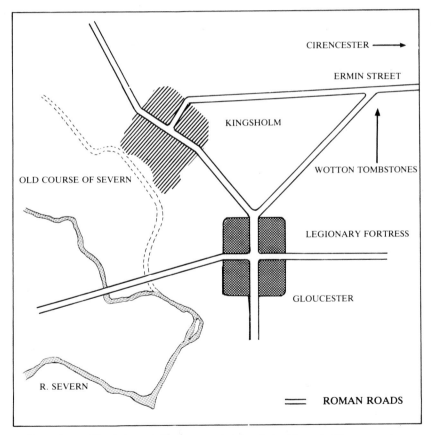

Military sites at Kingsholm and Gloucester and their relationship to the Wotton cemetery.

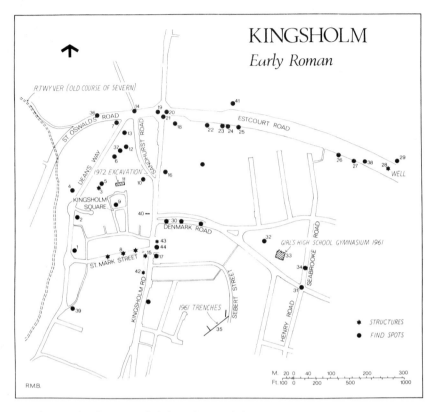

Distribution of early Roman finds from the Kingsholm area.

of the River Severn. Two phases of timber buildings have been identified along with first-century material extending over an area of about 20 hectares. Also found were pieces of military equipment, including a cheekpiece from a cavalryman's parade helmet. The type of unit which was housed within the fort or fortress is uncertain, and a number of different views are held by archaeologists. There are no finds from Kingsholm which identify the unit positively nor which show conclusively that it was legionary, auxiliary or a mixture of both. The cheekpiece might indicate the presence of auxiliary troops, but if the military buildings extended over as great an area as suggested, they would be too big to house the usual units of auxiliaries.

Two military tombstones have been found nearby at Wotton some 1.2km from Kingsholm. The first commemorates a cavalryman by the name of Rufus Sita who is shown in the carving riding down his enemy. He carries a shield on his left arm and a lance in his right hand. Above the carving in the

Part of a bronze cheekpiece from helmet found at Kingsholm.

Tombstone of Rufus Sita found at Wotton.

centre of the tombstone is a Sphinx with a lion on either side. The inscription reads:

> RVFVS SITA EQVES CHO VI
> TRACVM ANN XL STIP XXII
> HEREDES EXS TEST F CVRAVE
> H   S   E

which translated reads:

> Rufus Sita, trooper of the Sixth Cohort of Thracians,
> aged 40, of 22 years' service, lies buried here.
> His heirs had this erected according to the terms
> of his will.

An auxiliary cohort normally comprised only infantry, but as Rufus Sita is specifically referred to as '*eques*', that is a cavalryman or trooper, then the sixth cohort of Thracians must have been a unit comprising both infantry and cavalry, or what is known as a *cohors equitata*. Earlier in the first century this cohort was campaigning with the Fourteenth Legion, and it seems likely that it joined that legion when it sailed for Britain in A.D. 43.

The other tombstone found in Wotton in 1824 has been lost, but the inscription, which survived, was noted at the time and reads:

> XX S LIVI SATVRNINI STIPENDIORVM
> XIII ORVM MXXXX

> . . . soldier of the Twentieth Legion from
> the century of Livius Saturninus, of 13 years'
> service aged 40.

Assuming this latter tombstone to be genuine, it indicates that the Twentieth Legion was based in the area between leaving Colchester in A.D. 49-50 and arriving at Wroxeter in *c.* A.D. 64-66. It is very tempting to link this legion with the military installation found at Kingsholm, which excavation shows was vacated in the mid 60s. If the legionary tombstone found at Wotton is to be linked with Kingsholm then logically one must also associate the tombstone of Rufus Sita with the same site, showing that the unit based at Kingsholm was a mixed one comprising legionary and auxiliary troops, a phenomenon now shown to have been a regular feature in southern Britain during the first thirty years or so of Roman occupation.

GLOUCESTER

The limits of a legionary fortress occupying about 17.5 hectares have now been identified at Gloucester and a number of internal buildings excavated. The excavations conducted by M.W.C. Hassall and J.F. Rhodes in 1966-67 on the site of the New Market Hall were the first to reveal the plans of

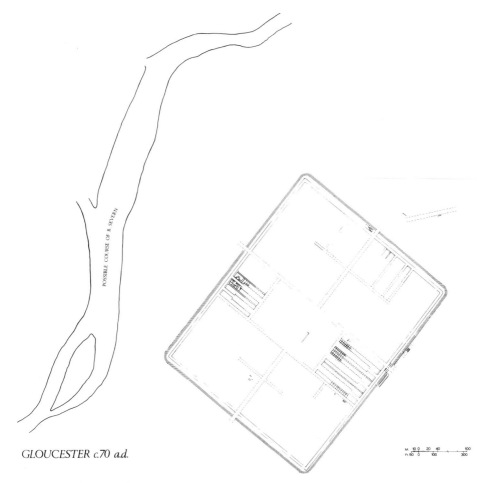

POSSIBLE COURSE OF R. SEVERN

GLOUCESTER c.70 a.d.

M. 10 0   20   40   100
Ft. 50 0   100   300

Plan of the legionary fortress at Gloucester.

buildings belonging to the fortress. Part of a barrack was found, the walls of which were built of clay on a timber framework. Some of the walls were plastered and the floors of the rooms covered with gravel or clay. In one of the partition walls of the barrack was a coin dated to A.D. 64-66, showing that it could not have been built before that date, assuming, of course, that this wall was not rebuilt at some stage. Pottery and coins from within the barrack indicated that occupation lasted until after A.D. 77-78. These dates were confirmed later by H. Hurst on the site of extensions to the Telephone Exchange, where excavations in 1969 revealed more timber-built barracks. These excavations along with others have enabled some of the internal

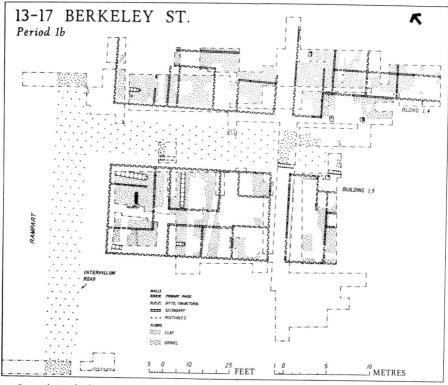

Barracks in the legionary fortress at Gloucester

layout of the fortress to be planned. The fortress was defended by a rampart which was at least 4m wide at its base and was revetted back and front with turves. In several places the rampart was found to contain courses of timber strapping to bind the material of the bank together. At various places around the circuit were timber towers built into the rampart, and around the outside was a V-shaped ditch about 2.5m wide at the top and at least 2m deep.

Excavations on the site of 45-49 Northgate Street in 1974 uncovered a building in the space between the rampart and the intervallum road. It measured 5m by 6.3m and was built of timber posts each about 15cms in diameter set into a trench. A gap in the south-east side of the building represents an entrance, which faced onto the *via praetoria*, that is the main road leading from the north gate to the headquarters buildings or *principia*. Carolyn Heighway, the excavator, interprets this structure as a guard-house for the garrison of the fortress north gate, which itself was not found. The posts of another structure were found to the north of the guard-house and these may have been for a timber stairway giving access to the rampart wall.

45-9 NORTHGATE STREET
GLOUCESTER 1974

Plan of Roman military features (period 1), first phase

Timber straping
for rampart

Structure 2

F 519

F 520

F 720

Rampart
PERIOD 1

Clay walls

Intervallum
street

F 705

F 701

Building 1

Timber guard-house inside north gate of Gloucester fortress.

The only evidence of a gate to the legionary fortress came when the site of 38-44 Eastgate Street was examined. Within the gate-tower of the *colonia* east gate were two earlier post-pits about 1m square and 1m deep which contained pieces of oak plank and lime wood. Clearly these pits were for the timber uprights of a gate and associated towers, but with only two posts it was not possible to be sure of the overall plan of the gate, although the excavators put forward their most likely interpretation.

In the central block across the fortress and in particular in the areas marked I and V on the plan the arrangement of barrack blocks has been

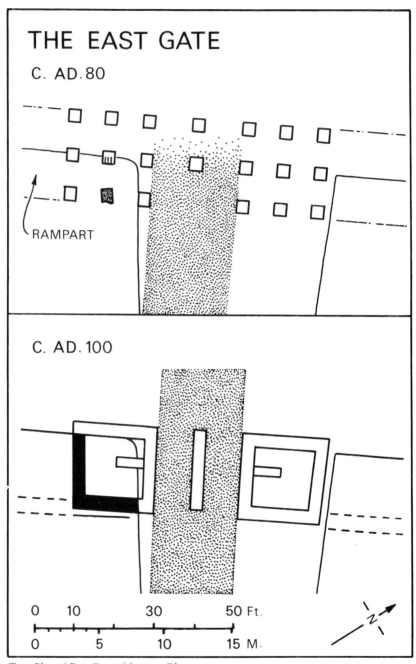

Top. Plan of East Gate of fortress, Gloucester.
Bottom. Plan of East Gate of COLONIA, Gloucester.

worked out from a series of excavations. In each case there were six barracks, sufficient for one of the ten cohorts of soldiers that made up a complete legion. The main streets of the fortress can be deduced, assuming the position of the gates, but in one or two places they have been found in excavations.

Which legion built the fortress and subsequently occupied it is uncertain. The dating evidence precludes the Twentieth Legion from being involved with the building of the Gloucester fortress, which does not appear to have started until after A.D. 64-66, by which time this legion was in Wroxeter. The most likely suggestion is that the Second Legion moved up from Exeter. Although recent excavations at Exeter have shown that some form of occupation continued within the fortress there until *c.* A.D. 75, this need not have involved the complete legion, and Exeter may have been held until the mid 70s while part of the legion, along with auxiliary troops, was detailed to Gloucester to construct a fortress for the entire legion to move into at a later date as part of the movement into South Wales in A.D. 75. A tile-stamp of the Second Legion in Gloucester Museum is unlikely to have come from a first-century fortress at Gloucester as these stamps were not used in Britain until later in the second century. A more recent suggestion that the Fourteenth Legion built Gloucester in A.D. 69 and occupied it for a year before leaving Britain in A.D. 70 hardly seems likely.

OTHER SITES

At Rodborough a ditch 4.3m wide and 2m deep was traced for at least 76m during excavations and observations of builders' trenches. It had a military look in that it was V-shaped and the mid-first-century pottery associated with it indicated that it was the correct date for a fort ditch. However, on this evidence alone it would be unwise to be dogmatic about the presence or otherwise of a fort on Rodborough Common.

Three parallel ditches plus early pottery and coins have suggested to some that Roman military remains are to be found in the village of Dymock 19kms north-west of Gloucester, but, as at Rodborough, the evidence is far from conclusive, and until further work is done we shall have to keep an open mind on these two sites.

More and more of the towns and villages of Roman Britain are showing that their presence in a particular spot was due to the Roman army having established forts there. For this reason a number of people have suggested that Dorn, Bourton-on-the-Water and White Walls were sites of forts during the first century, but there is no evidence to support this argument and for the moment it must remain as speculation. Similarly the presence of early Roman material at Kingscote does not prove that the Roman army was stationed there.

The Ermin Street Guard.

2
The Cities of Gloucester and Cirencester

As the Roman army moved across the country, areas were handed over to the civilian authorities to be organised in such a way as to develop the economy, maintain law and order and, perhaps foremost in the eyes of those in charge, to romanise the native population. The Roman answer to these problems was to create urban settlements, towns and cities, like those that already existed in other parts of the Roman Empire. The highest ranking of these was the *colonia*, specifically established to accommodate retired army veterans, and such a settlement was built to replace the legionary fortress at Gloucester. Here the native population saw a city developing along the lines of Rome upon whose charter the *colonia* of Gloucester modelled its own. The city itself, however, took no part in the daily administration of the *civitas* or tribal area. For this purpose the authorities preferred to utilise the existing tribal structure, and in each area they planted a town to act as the centre for local government, trade, entertainment, education and law. Frequently such towns replaced earlier forts and their *vici* or extra-mural settlements, mainly because much of the land was already in Roman hands and there was consequently less need to confiscate further and risk alienating local landowners. The vacant military fort at Cirencester with some additional land was thus chosen for the site of the administrative centre of the *Dobunni*.

The occasion for the founding of towns was dependent upon the military situation. In the east of England sizeable towns were in existence by the time of the rebellion headed by Queen Boudicca in A.D. 60-1 as excavations at Colchester, London and Verulamium have shown. In the west, however, the army stayed longer and, as we have seen in the previous chapter, did not leave Gloucester and Cirencester until the late 70s or even slightly later. It follows, therefore, that towns in *Dobunni* territory were established at least a quarter of a century later than those founded in eastern England.

Once established, settlements acquired names, and although we have no direct evidence as to how they originated scholars are able to work out possible derivations. The full name for Gloucester may have been COLONIA NERVIA GLEVENSIS (or Colonia Nerviana Glevensium) as two inscriptions discussed later indicate. The name is also mentioned on a military diploma and in the Antonine Itinerary (see Chapter 6) where the G has been miscopied to a C. Whatever the full title, it is clear from all these sources that the Roman name for the city was GLEVUM; this seems to have come from a native word meaning 'bright', and hence means 'bright place or bright town'. After the Roman period the name is written in various ways including *Cair Gloui* and *Gleawcaester* in the Anglo-Saxon Chronicle, leading eventually to Gloucester.

The Roman name for Cirencester is not recorded on any contemporary inscription from Britain but only in Ptolemy's Geography and the Ravenna Cosmography, the former being compiled in Alexandria in the second quarter of the second century A.D. and the latter by an anonymous cleric of Ravenna in the late seventh century. It is not clear how the name *Corinium* came about, although it may be derived from a British word connected with trees and was possibly the name of the tribal centre at Bagendon before being transferred to the Roman fort on the banks of the River Churn.

Public Works

GLOUCESTER

The birthplace of a soldier of the Sixth Legion is recorded on a tombstone found in Rome as NER GLEVI, and it is generally agreed that this stands for NERVIA GLEVENSIUM, which indicates that Gloucester (*Glevum*) was founded during the reign of the Emperor Nerva (A.D. 96-8). A late first-century date for the founding of the *colonia* is also indicated by the archaeological evidence because the buildings which lay directly upon the destroyed legionary fortress, that is those of the *colonia*, contained coins dated to after A.D. 87 in their construction levels. These early buildings were found at the 13-17 Berkeley Street excavations and again at 10 Eastgate Street, and were clearly not constructed until the last decade of the first century A.D. Their plan closely resembles the plans of the barracks found in the earlier legionary fortress with slight differences in the internal division of the overall block and, in some cases, the addition of a verandah. The reason for the similarity in plan may be due to the involvement of the Roman army in the initial planning and construction of the *colonia*. An inscribed stone found at 41-51 Eastgate Street supports this idea as it is a centurial building stone of the sort which was built into structures erected by the army. The inscription is not complete, but the top line begins CO, presumably the beginning of COHORT with its number and, possibly, name following below.

The rampart of the legionary fortress was still standing when the *colonia* was constructed, for it was incorporated in its defences. The front of the rampart was cut back and a stone wall about 1.5m wide was inserted. Within these defences, apart from the barrack-like buildings, little else of the first

A tombstone found in Rome which records the name of Gloucester.

phase of the *colonia* has been found. Some walls of what must have been the forum and basilica have been examined in *insula* III. These walls were unusually narrow for such a building causing the excavator, H. Hurst, to interpret them as sleeper walls for timber colonnades. Some idea of the internal decoration at this time can be gleaned from the fragments of imported and Purbeck marble found. Little dating evidence came from these early levels, but on stratigraphical grounds it is clear that they are from the late first century and represent the walls of the original forum and basilica. At some time during the first half of the second century this building was replaced by a more substantial structure consisting of colonnaded ranges surrounding a sandstone paved courtyard. In the courtyard was a rectangular foundation which may have been the base for a statue. There are no other plans of public buildings that once existed in Gloucester, such as the baths or theatre, but there are substantial remains indicating their presence. One such building stood to the north-west of the forum where large columns,

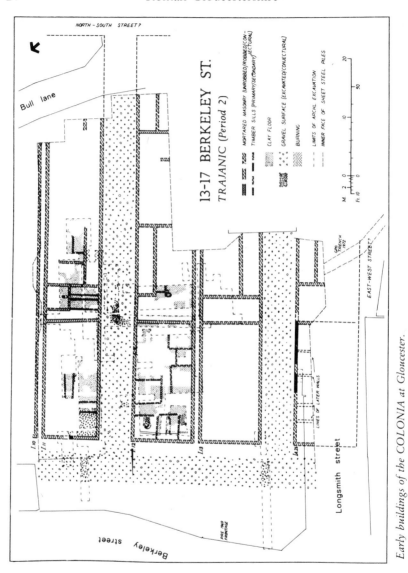

Early buildings of the COLONIA at Gloucester.

hypocausts and lead piping suggest the possible site for the public baths. Columns have been found at various times in Westgate Street and, as they are some way from a known Roman street, they must have been associated with a building rather than part of a street colonnade. One possibility is that they belonged to a temple, but they appear rather large and too widely spaced for such an interpretation. Various pieces of sculpture have been discovered, indicating the existence of temples.

An inscribed stone found at 41-51 Eastgate Street, Gloucester, possibly recording a cohort of the Roman army.

As is the case with most of the towns in Roman Britain a great deal has been learnt about the defences of Gloucester in the past decade, and the story turns out to be more complicated than hitherto believed. As described above, the original *colonia* was defended by inserting a narrow stone wall in front of the legionary rampart, thus enclosing some 17.5 hectares. Late in the second century the rampart behind this wall was raised, and at the same time stone towers were built into it. During the third century the stone wall was rebuilt except for a stretch of about 30m on each side of the gates which was not replaced until the fourth century. When this was done it is likely that the external towers were built, one of which was found and excavated north-east of East Gate. It was rectangular in plan and, like the fourth-century wall, built of large re-used blocks of building stone, supported on a rubble foundation with timber piles beneath.

Excavations in 1974 recovered details of the North and East Gates. They

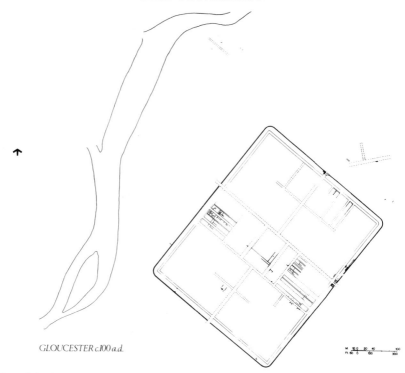

GLOUCESTER c.100 a.d.

Plan of the COLONIA at Gloucester in the late first century.

differ in plan and the North Gate, a free-standing L-shaped structure to which the *colonia* wall had been added, may be earlier than the foundation of the *colonia*. The timber structures found on this site (45-9 Northgate Street) behind the military rampart were replaced by a stone building (no. 4) on the same alignment. It measured 14m by 6m and had six rooms, one large one at the north end, three leading off a corridor and a narrow room across the front of the building. It is thought that it served the same function as its timber predecessor and was a guard-house for the gate. It was demolished to make way for the addition of the earth rampart at the end of the second century. The late-Roman city wall was also found on this site, although much of its upper part had been robbed. Three courses of large oolite blocks about 30cms thick were resting on a mortar and oolite foundation which was laid on vertical oak piles driven into the natural sand. The East Gate was found during the excavations at 38-44 Eastgate Street where the same sequence in the defences was noted and where valuable dating evidence was recovered. In places the wall was standing to a height of about 2m. The gate consisted of two square towers and two passageways.

The Roman defences at Gloucester can be summarised as follows:-

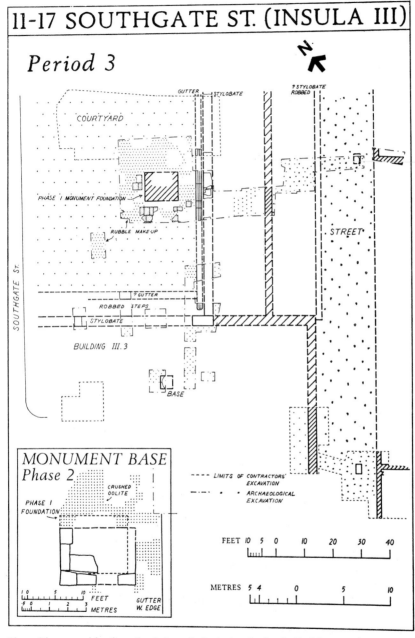

11-17 SOUTHGATE ST. (INSULA III)

Period 3

N

COURTYARD

GUTTER   STYLOBATE

? STYLOBATE ROBBED

PHASE I MONUMENT FOUNDATION

RUBBLE MAKE-UP

STREET

SOUTHGATE ST.

? GUTTER

ROBBED STEPS

STYLOBATE

BUILDING III.3

BASE

MONUMENT BASE
Phase 2

CRUSHED OOLITE

PHASE I FOUNDATION

---- LIMITS OF CONTRACTORS' EXCAVATION

— • ARCHAEOLOGICAL EXCAVATION

1 0   5   10 FEET
-5 0   1   2   3 METRES

GUTTER
W. EDGE

FEET 10 5 0   10   20   30   40

METRES 5 4   0   5   10

Plan of forum and basilica after being rebuilt during the first half of the second century.

Late 60s A.D.	Legionary Fortress — earth rampart with timber gates and towers.
Late 90s	First *colonia* defences — stone wall inserted in front of legionary rampart.
Late second century	Earth bank added to existing one — stone towers built.
Third century	Wall rebuilt except for 30m stretches either side of the gates.
Mid fourth century	Wall either side of gates rebuilt, projecting towers added.

The layout of the *colonia* streets was dictated by the position of the gates and was similar to that inside the fortress. Some of the streets were colonnaded and were served by sewers and drains, which carried away waste from the city to be discharged into the river. By the beginning of the second century, the *colonia* was established, streets were laid out and its defences organised. Some of the official buildings were finished and others, no doubt, were still under construction. A municipal tilery was in operation by the 120s, stamping its tiles RPG (REI PUBLICAE GLEVENSIUM) and leaving no doubt that by this date the city was firmly established.

CIRENCESTER

There are no epigraphic or literary sources which help us to pin down a precise date for the foundation of the town, as there are at Gloucester. Compared with what happened there, the army had little effect on the layout of the tribal capital. The line of Ermin Street was maintained and must have dictated the orientation of the town's street grid, but the rest of the military features had been deliberately removed from view and had no effect on the later town plan, as the subsidence of the basilica into the earlier fort ditch shows. The buildings which once stood in the *vicus* were also cleared away when the streets were laid out in the last quarter of the first century. It was at this time that work started on the civic centre, consisting of forum and basilica, which was at the heart of the town (*insula I*) and dominated the townscape. The cathedral-like basilica was 100m long and 24m wide, being divided internally into a nave 10m wide with flanking aisles, each 5.5m. The south-west end of the nave terminated in an apse, but there is no indication of one at the other end, and, if we can believe the plan of excavations and observations produced by Cripps in 1898, a second apse looks unlikely. On the south-east side of this great hall was a range of rooms for official purposes. Imported marble was used as a veneer to decorate the walls, and mouldings of Purbeck marble have been found from within the basilica. It is not surprising that a building which stood for something like 400 years needed regular repair and maintenance work. In the middle of the

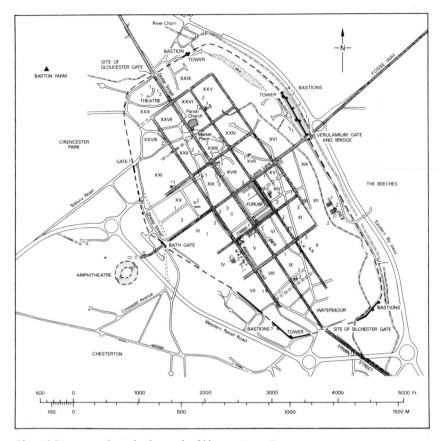

Plan of Cirencester from the first to the fifth centuries A.D.

second century major structural work was carried out, as it had begun to subside into the earlier fort ditch, and further alterations and repairs have been noted.

On the north-west side of the basilica was the forum, consisting of an open courtyard or piazza 108m by 68m surrounded on all sides by a colonnade. Little of it has been excavated, but the walls which have been found fit the traditional plan of a Romano-British forum. In the fourth century a wall was built across the piazza, dividing it into two parts, and at about the same time the north-west wing was modified and a mosaic was laid in the colonnade. It has been suggested that these alterations were a direct result of Cirencester becoming the capital of one of the provinces into which Britain was divided towards the end of the second century A.D. Indeed an inscription found in 1891 in a garden in Victoria Road comes from a Jupiter column restored by the 'governor of Britannia Prima', and it seems

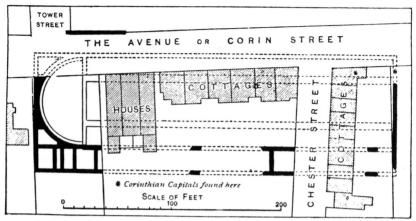

Plan of W. Cripp's excavation of the basilica at Cirencester, 1897-8.

very likely that Cirencester was the residence of the governor and the provincial capital. At what point in the fourth century the alterations were made is not yet known, but they may have been connected, as Mr. Wacher thinks, with the conversion of part of the forum to the governor's *praetorium* or palace.

The construction of the civic centre and of the town's streets took place at about the same time. Indeed it may be argued that the streets would have preceeded any major building programme so that the transporting of stone from quarries could be accomplished more easily. On the other hand, temporary metalled tracks may have been laid for this purpose, and such early road surfaces have been found on a different alignment from the street grid just to the south of the basilica. Streets were laid out in straight lines and at right angles to each other, forming rectangular blocks of land *(insulae)* averaging about 158m by 100m. They varied in width from 6-9m and even 12m near the town's centre, and were drained. Alongside the main streets were colonnades, or covered footpaths, separated from the street by regularly-spaced columns supporting the roof over the path. The quantity of stone required for these streets and official buildings was considerable, and before construction work could begin suitable limestone had to be located and extracted. The nearest source which could be quarried relatively easily lay to the west of the town in an area now known as the Querns. Here are the widespread tell-tale signs of quarrying, mounds and hollows representing quarries and waste dumps, although not all are necessarily Roman.

Naturally, when a site was sought for the town's amphitheatre, it was to the waste land of the disused quarries that the town council turned. The quarry waste, consisting of limestone brash and clay, was heaped into banks

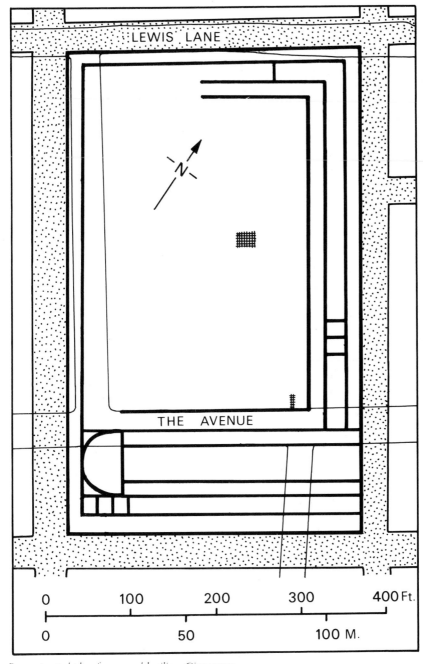

LEWIS LANE

THE AVENUE

| 0 | 100 | 200 | 300 | 400 Ft. |

| 0 | 50 | 100 M. |

Reconstructed plan forum and basilica, Cirencester.

Inscription from the base of a Jupiter column, Cirencester.

and shaped into the familiar elliptical structure of an amphitheatre. The banks formed the base for seats and were partly interrupted on the line of the main axis of the amphitheatre to provide entrances to the arena, which itself measured 41m across and was 49m long. The seating bank was terraced by small dry-stone walls upon which people stood or sat, perhaps on wooden planks. Excavation of this feature in 1966 showed that originally there were at least thirty rows of seats, which, assuming they continued all the way round the bank, could accommodate somewhere in the region of 6,000 people. There is no evidence as to the type of events which took place, but gladiators were to be found in Britain and these may have entertained the local population at Cirencester. Otherwise, less glamorous activities such as wrestling or even bear-baiting were the normal programme. Shows were

Ermin Street in the foreground and a colonnade wall in the background, with a fallen column in front.

paid for by local magistrates at election-time and on subsequent religious or political festivals. The amphitheatre was also used as an assembly point where most of the adult population of the town could hear speeches from their own leaders or visiting officials of the governor's retinue, or even from the governor himself. One can also imagine that on market days, when many farmers were in town, shows were put on, perhaps not unlike the fairs that were associated with medieval markets.

A less robust form of entertainment was to be found in the theatre, where drama, mime and recitation were the main forms of activity. The curving walls found in *insula* XXX must be considered as belonging to the theatre which Cirencester surely possessed. Often associated with the theatre was a temple. So far no structural remains have been found which could be so interpreted, but various architectural fragments and pieces of sculpture indicate that it existed. There are representations of Mercury, Minerva, Cupid and Diana as well as a number of local Celtic gods and goddesses.

As far as we know, the city of Cirencester was not defended until the end of the second century, one hundred years later than Gloucester, when the built-up area was surrounded by an earth rampart and ditches. Before the bank was erected, stone gates and towers were constructed. Two gates have been found belonging to this period: the Verulamium Gate and the Bath Gate. Only part of the Verulamium Gate was found by Mr. Wacher in 1960,

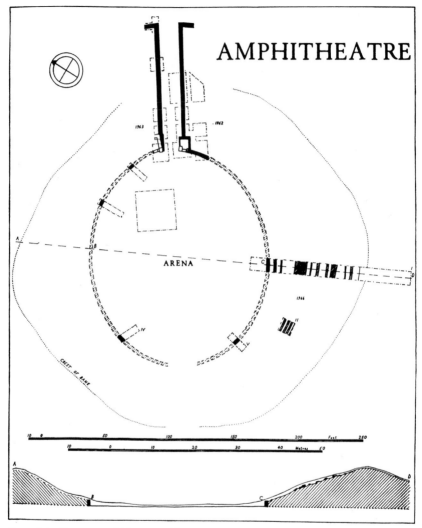

Plan of the Roman amphitheatre at Cirencester.

but the behaviour of the bridge abutment and other details have enabled him to produce a complete plan which postulates four portals of about the same size, each one capable, judging from the ruts which were found, of allowing wheeled vehicles to pass through. On either side were projecting towers, and a bridge carried the road to Verulamium (St. Albans) across the River Churn. The Bath Gate found in 1974 was of a similar plan but with only two portals. Embedded in the late second-century earth bank were square towers, two of which have so far been found. So by the beginning of the

View across the seating bank of the Cirencester amphitheatre.

third century a visitor approaching Cirencester would have seen a town surrounded by an earth bank, monumental stone gates spanning the main roads and stone towers spaced regularly along the rampart. During the first half of the third century the earth rampart was cut back and a stone wall 1.2m wide was inserted. In some places it was found necessary to replace this wall with a wider one. The only other modification to the defences that has been detected took place in the middle of the fourth century when external towers were added to the front of the wall. The plan of the foundations for these towers is of two sorts, one rectangular and the other polygonal. The stones found in association with the rectangular foundations indicate that the superstructure built on them was also polygonal. The area enclosed by these defences was about ninety-six hectares, but it is by no

Seating arrangements in the Cirencester amphitheatre.

means certain that all of the land inside was completely occupied by buildings, and there are indications that some quite large areas were not built on for several centuries and that other areas remained permanently empty. However, as the sample so far excavated only represents a small fraction of the ninety-six hectares, it is unwise to make categorical statements at this stage of research.

Houses and Shops

Along with the construction of streets and public buildings there was a need to provide housing and shops. Our knowledge of early private buildings in most Romano-British towns is very scant and rarely has it been possible to draw complete plans of buildings from the lowest levels of towns. In both

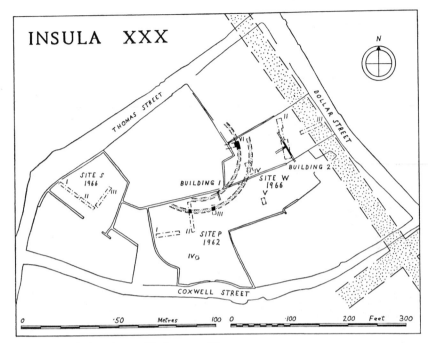

Reconstructed plan of a possible theatre at Cirencester.

Gloucester and Cirencester the ground level rose some 2-3m during the Roman period and a further 3m or so after; consequently the earliest structures are buried deep. Occasionally archaeological trenches have reached them, but the large areas needed to recover complete plans of the first houses and shops have not generally been available for excavation. As well as the depth, there is another problem relating to the preservation of shops from such early levels, due in part to their position in the town. Commercial property required a good position along the more populous streets, and frequent changing of hands resulted in rebuilding or extensions. This continual rebuilding on the same site caused damage to the earlier structures beneath. When, therefore, it is possible to open up large areas and to excavate them down to the earliest buildings, very often their remains are fragmentary and difficult to piece together. Despite all these limitations however, it is possible to say something about the beginnings of some houses and shops in both Gloucester and Cirencester.

GLOUCESTER

Reference has already been made to the unusual plan of the first *colonia* buildings and the fact that they resembled the earlier legionary barracks. The

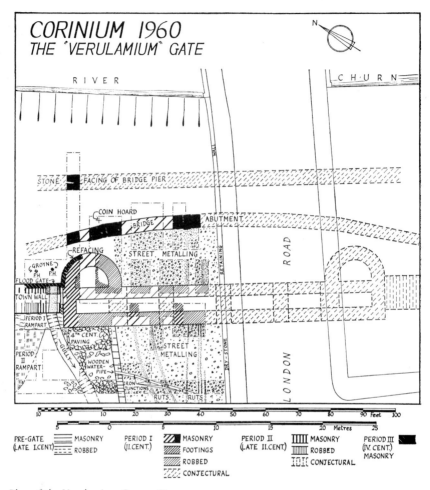

Plan of the Verulamium Gate at Cirencester.

excavations at 13-17 Berkeley Street showed details of these buildings and those which replaced them, and the information obtained from this site can be used to illustrate some of the general changes that were taking place to Roman houses in Gloucester. The external walls of the first *colonia* buildings were constructed on sleeper walls of stone and clay which terminated at floor level. Along with the evidence of the keying on the back of the wall-plaster, this points to the use of timber and clay, or clay blocks on their own, for the building's superstructure. Internal divisions were constructed mainly on timber beams although occasionally shallow stone walls were noted. Floors were generally made of clay, and one of them, in building I,

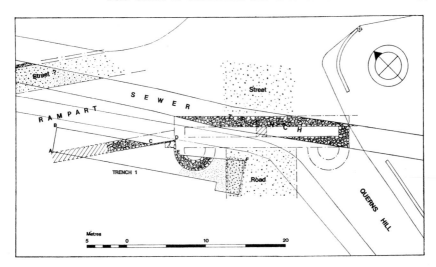

The south-west, or Bath Gate, at Cirencester.

12, sealed a coin of A.D. 87 which, taken together with other material found, indicates that these structures belonged to the *colonia* and were not the last remnants of the legionary fortress. During the second or third decades of the second century these buildings in *insula* I were replaced by structures which H. Hurst believes were constructed by private means. Building I, 14 is such an example, a small compact unit measuring about 12m by 11m with walls built of mortared masonry about 50-60cms wide. Floors were made of pebbly mortar or dirty clay, and in the south-west corner room was a tiled hearth, of which one of the tiles was stamped RPG indicating that originally it had come from the municipal tilery and was probably being re-used in a private dwelling. Small-scale industrial processes, including iron-working and pottery-making, were noted in the proximity of this building. An updraught kiln was found to the east of I, 14 and pottery from the vicinity included part of a lamp chimney and a *mortaria* with an illiterate stamp.

Mr. Wacher has suggested that these changes in building plan and use might reflect a veteran acquiring sufficient wealth to be able to buy a villa in the *territorium* outside the noisey and crowded town, and replacing his town house with a smaller version, in which commercial activities could be undertaken on his behalf. There is no direct evidence to support this attractive idea, but clearly the structures which were replacing the original *colonia* buildings could not accommodate as many people, and this might indicate a movement of people out of an over-crowded town into more spacious surroundings in the countryside. Whatever the case may be, by the

Reconstructed drawing of the Bath Gate, Cirencester.

middle of the second century this small house (I, 14) and others were replaced by a sophisticated and sizeable stone courtyard house (I, 18) continuing the trend of low-density building. This building consisted of a block 30m square occupying a corner plot between two streets with an eastwards extension along one of the street frontages, the limits of which have not been traced. In the centre of the main block was a paved courtyard about 8m square and linked to the street to the south by a 3m wide passageway. There may also have been an entrance to the street on the west. A series of foundations in the courtyard have been interpreted as the base for a fountain and water cistern. All four of its sides were flanked by ranges of

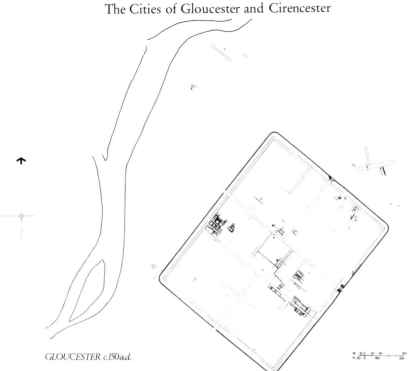

GLOUCESTER c.150a.d.

Plan of the Gloucester COLONIA in the middle of the second century A.D.

rooms, most of which were floored with mortar on pitched rubble foundations. However, room 9, the largest room and situated in the centre of the east range, had a mosaic floor and is likely to have been a *triclinium*. Very few examples of this type of house-plan have been found in Britain, but it has many parallels in other parts of the Roman world, particularly in Italy, and it would be interesting to know whether this is a unique example in Gloucester. If it was the only building constructed in this way at the beginning of the second century, then the owner was probably somebody of importance, perhaps an official coming from abroad and working in Gloucester. At the beginning of the third century this dignified house was deliberately taken down and its material salvaged for future use. Most of the site then remained vacant throughout the rest of the Roman period. To the south, extensive alterations were taking place in the late second century with most of the buildings being equipped with mosaic floors, indicating that the custom of having such floors was only becoming fashionable towards the end of the second century, just at the time when building I, 18 with its one mosaic was coming to its end.

During the excavations at the New Market Hall in 1966-7 the early *colonia* buildings were again found, but their subsequent history is different from

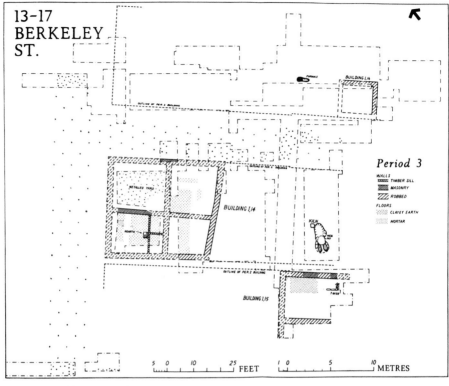

Plan of building 1,14, Gloucester.

that of those already described. Some were replaced in stone during the Hadrianic period (*c.* A.D. 117-138), but others were abandoned during the second quarter of the second century. In the fourth century one of the masonry buildings was found to be encroaching on to the street it was fronting, possibly indicating that land was at a premium. The same building was quite elaborately decorated inside. It had at least three mosaics, of which the one in the main central room, dated to the fourth century, contained a panel depicting Bacchus riding on a panther. Fragments of another figured mosaic were found in the easternmost room, in which there were also considerable amounts of brightly-coloured fallen wall-plaster. After this period of prosperity the building seems to have been allowed to decay, suggesting that the original owners had moved out or fallen on hard times. Even so the excavators detected some form of occupation extending into the fifth and possibly sixth century, and there is no reason why people could not have been living in the shells of these once-sumptuous buildings until the town fell to the Saxons in A.D. 577.

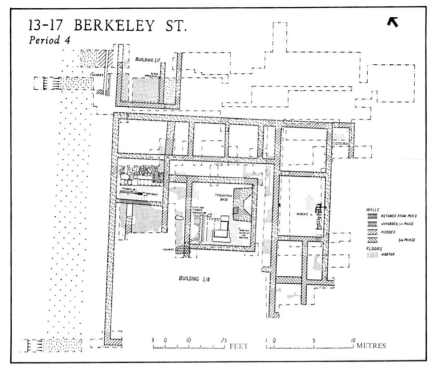

13-17 BERKELEY ST.
Period 4

BUILDING 1,17

CULVERT

CISTERN

FOUNTAIN BASE

MOSAIC

WALLS
 RETAINED FROM PER 3
 UNROBBED, 1st PHASE
 ROBBED
  2nd PHASE
FLOORS
 MORTAR

BUILDING 1,18

5 0 10   25   FEET   1 0   5   10 METRES

Plan of building 1,18, Gloucester.

Although numerous chance discoveries of individual items have been made over the past two centuries in Gloucester, such as mosaics, architectural fragments and other finds, indicating the quality of the buildings and their internal decoration, there are no plans of buildings (other than those already described) which contribute significantly to our understanding of the houses and shops within the city walls.

Outside the walls a thriving community seems to have developed by the mid-second century. Some people were concerned with small industrial activities such as pottery-making and iron-working, and presumably other 'unsocial occupations' were relegated to these areas. Evidence for a Roman quay on the banks of the River Severn was claimed way back in 1849 when a wall made of Forest of Dean stones about 1m square was found and reported to be supported on piles. Similar observations were made in 1973. Buildings associated with the docks must have stood close to the quay and one can imagine a bustling settlement in this quarter. Outside the North Gate a monumental arcaded structure has been found which may have been part of a public market, and in 1971 J. Rhodes found a series of buildings lining the road to Cirencester. A most striking edifice would have been the arch

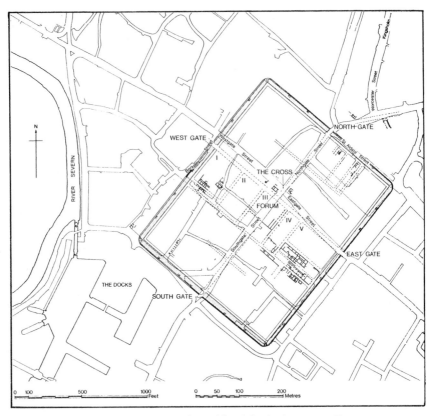

Plan of the Gloucester COLONIA in the middle of the third century A.D.

straddling the road outside the gate. The foundations of this were discovered by A.P. Garrod in 1977. Although little of the extra-mural settlement has been investigated and its limits have not been defined, it can be seen clearly that outside the walls of *Glevum* there was a densely-built-up area occupying almost certainly two or more times the area within. If this is added to the city itself then the total occupied area of approximately forty hectares is comparable with the other *coloniae* of Roman Britain and of a reasonable size in relation to its neighbour, Cirencester.

CIRENCESTER

A row of shops in *insula* V is dated to the last quarter of the first century and must be more or less contemporary with the building of the forum and basilica. They were of wattle and daub on timber framework and some walls, particularly in the domestic quarters, were plastered and painted. Gradually the timber was replaced by stone, shop by shop, indicating

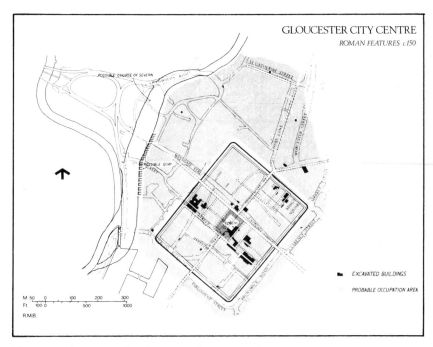

The extent of extra mural settlement at Gloucester in about A.D. 150.

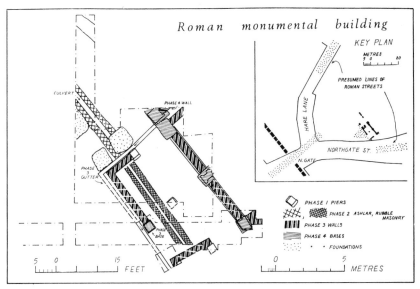

A monumental building found outside the North Gate at Gloucester.

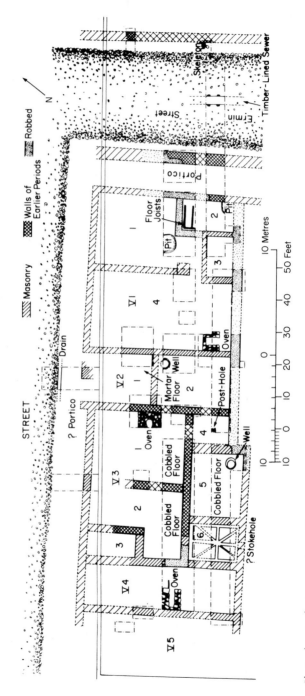

Shops close to the town centre at Cirencester.

individual ownership. By the fourth century, five shop units can be recognised with domestic accommodation attached which included, in one case, under-floor heating. There were also ovens and wells in this complex, but nothing to indicate the commodities being dealt with.

Further south-east on the other side of Ermin Street (*insula* VI), a series of buildings was found between 1974-6 which are best interpreted as shops. The rear part of a timber building with good quality floors was uncovered which at the end of the second century was cleared away to make room for a public building (VI, 1). The sequence of stone buildings found to the south of VI, 1 was not completely excavated and therefore extremely difficult to unravel. The earliest levels investigated in any detail were dated to the third century, and the plan of each building uncovered was very like the rear quarters of shops which stretched back from Ermin Street. Three distinct units can be seen. Building VI, 6 had a side entrance leading from a yard into an entrance porch from which one gained access to other rooms, the largest of which at the rear seems to have been the principal living room. It had a well-made *opus signinum* floor with quarter-round mouldings against each wall which were themselves decorated with painted plaster. Sufficient space existed between these private rooms and Ermin Street for the business part of the premises. By the fourth century this shop and its yard had been replaced by another, much larger stone building with a mosaic corridor and room on its south side (VI, 3). Without knowing the arrangement of the rooms in the front part of the shop it would be unwise to speculate about the details of possible amalgamation of properties into larger units, although there are indications that this occurred. Even though it was only possible to examine the latest levels in *insula* VI, it is clear that in the heart of the town, along the colonnaded Ermin Street, shops were tightly packed together, having a narrow street frontage and extending backwards some way. In between there were alleys and yards. The discovery of mosaics in some rooms of the residential parts of these shops suggests that their owners were not short of money.

Mosaic floors were not restricted to private houses, but the discovery of so many over the past two hundred years may be taken as an indication of the number and style of houses in *Corinium*. One discovery which must have caught the attention of most of Cirencester occurred in 1849 when, during the digging of trenches for sewers in Dyer street, mosaic floors, wall-plaster and hypocausts were uncovered. Eventually, with the backing of Earl Bathurst, two floors were removed from the ground and relaid in a purpose-built museum erected by the Earl. It now seems clear that other mosaics found close by in 1783 and 1820 came from the same building (XVII, 1) and the fact that at least four magnificently-designed and well-made mosaic floors have come from the same house makes it rather special and arguably the most elegantly 'carpeted' town house ever found in Roman

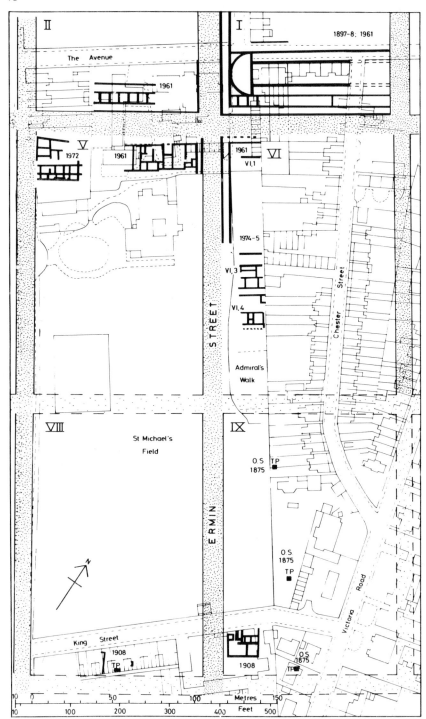

The area to the south and west of the basilica at Cirencester.

An engraving from the ILLUSTRATED LONDON NEWS showing the lifting of the Hunting Dogs mosaics in Cirencester, 1849.

Britain. As several of the mosaics date to the second century and one, the Orpheus pavement, to the fourth, it looks as though the fourth-century owners had new floors laid as well as keeping the earlier ones. The position of these remains in *insula* XVII suggests that they were part of one wing of a much larger house which may have occupied the entire north-west corner plot of the *insula*. In 1922, when a well was being dug in the garden of a bungalow under construction in Victoria Road, parts of three mosaics from a private house were found and fortunately were accurately recorded at the

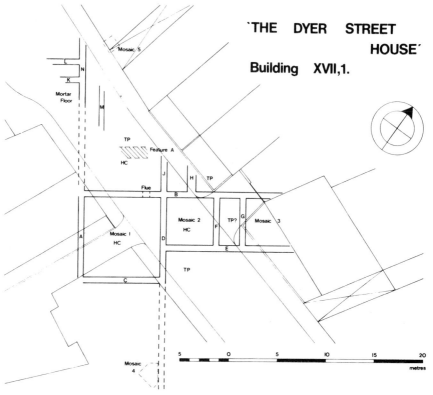

Plan of the Roman house found in Dyer Street in 1849, building XVII, 1.

time. Also found from the same building were tiles stamped with various groups of letters, which are discussed later.

The main advance in our knowledge of houses is due to the work of the Cirencester Excavation Committee from 1958 until the present day. In some of the sites examined conditions have not been ideal for controlled excavation; a number have had to be abandoned because of lack of time and on occasions the area allowed for excavation has not enabled much sense to be made out of the remains. However, some general observations can be made. Towards the end of the first century A.D. and during the second, houses were being built in limestone with little use being made of tile or brick in the walls themselves, its use being restricted to roofs and hypocausts. Quite early on walls were plastered and decorated and gradually, during the second century, houses were provided with mosaic floors. Some had their own bath suites and many had underfloor heating in their principal rooms. This could be achieved in two ways. The first method was to lower the floor level in the room and then to build regularly-spaced pillars of tile or stone so that larger

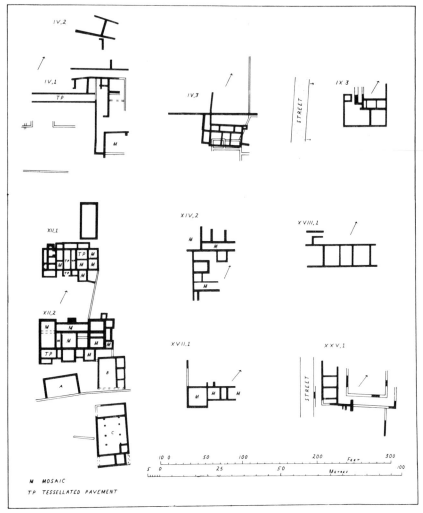

Plans of houses found in Cirencester.

tiles places on the top of each pillar formed a continuous base on which to
build a floor. Around the room flues were set into the walls to draw air from
beneath the floor and out into the atmosphere. A fire was made in a flue to
one side of the room and below floor level which could be attended to from
an outside stokehole. By regulating the flues in the wall the air could be
drawn across the fire, become heated and then circulate beneath the floor.
Some heat would also radiate from the flues in the wall and gradually the
stone and tile of the walls and floor would act not unlike modern storage

A reconstructed Roman kitchen in the Corinium Museum.

heaters. The fire could be controlled to provide a comfortable temperature for the occupants of the house. Another method of underfloor heating, which seems to replace the 'pillared hypocaust', is usually referred to as the channelled hypocaust (or sometimes the Union Jack hypocaust because of the pattern). Here the hot air is made to circulate beneath the floor by a series of channels leading from the fire.

Before 1970 three sites from within the Roman town had produced significant remains of houses, but in none of them was it possible to trace the development of a house from its beginnings: they were at Parsonage Field, Watermoor, (now occupied by Watermoor Clinic) where a maze of walls, mainly of a fourth-century house, were uncovered in 1957-9 (*insula* IV); 18 The Avenue where part of a courtyard house (XIV, 2) was found, and finally beneath the Saxon and abbey churches, where the disjointed remains of another courtyard house were located and planned (XXV, 1). All of these, along with other house remains, are shown on page 51 where it can be seen that, despite all the attention paid to Cirencester's past, little is known of the history of the town house in *Corinium*. With this in mind, when the well-preserved remains of a group of Roman buildings were discovered on the Beeches Road allotments and threatened by work connected with the ring road, the Cirencester Excavation Committee, together with the Department

Artist's reconstruction of building XII, 1 found in Beeches Road.

of the Environment, undertook large-scale excavations between 1970-3.

The latest phases of two, or possibly three, houses were uncovered and examined in detail (*insula* XII, 1 and 2). In one or two limited places it was possible to explore beneath the stone buildings to see if earlier ones existed, but all the indications are that this part of the town remained free of building until the middle or late fourth century. The plot lay just inside the eastern defences and appears to have been subjected to flooding during the Roman period. Whether the stream which borders the west of the site was there in Roman times is uncertain, but, as now, it was very low lying and would have acted as a natural drain for excess water. Building XII, 1 was constructed originally as a rectangular block measuring 14.5m by 9.5m externally with some six rooms and corridors. Gradually throughout the later part of the fourth century, and possibly even in the fifth century, rooms were added on all sides. To the west a bath suite was built, containing a changing room (15) with mosaic floor, a cold room (14) with a flagged floor and cold plunge bath attached (13) and two heated rooms with a possible hot bath (10 & 12). There were two flues or stokeholes providing heat for the two warm rooms, which had been constructed in a room of the original house (9) and were therefore within the building itself. In one of the flues was found a damaged statue of *Fortuna*. The rooms added to the north had the appearance of service rooms and one (3) was probably a kitchen. To the east two rooms, probably bedrooms, were built on, each one provided with a simple mosaic

The hare mosaic as excavated. Note that the top panel has been reconstructed the other way up in the Corinium Museum.

consisting of a red rectangle surrounded by white *tesserae*. Room 19 originally had a mosaic and was most probably the main room of the house, but at some stage in the late fourth century was considered too small for the owner's needs and so a hole was made in the room's south wall and an extension built. A mosaic was laid over the breached wall and in the extension. Differences in workmanship and style, as well as the frequent use of yellow *tesserae* in the extension which are not present in room 19, indicate that the floors were laid at different times, but expertly joined together. This was not to be the end of alterations to the main room of the house, for central heating was later installed, consisting of limestone blocks mortared together and arranged so as to form a channelled hypocaust. There is evidence to suggest that another mosaic floor was laid on top of the blocks, and the hypocaust undoubtedly functioned, as the 'hare' mosaic was stained

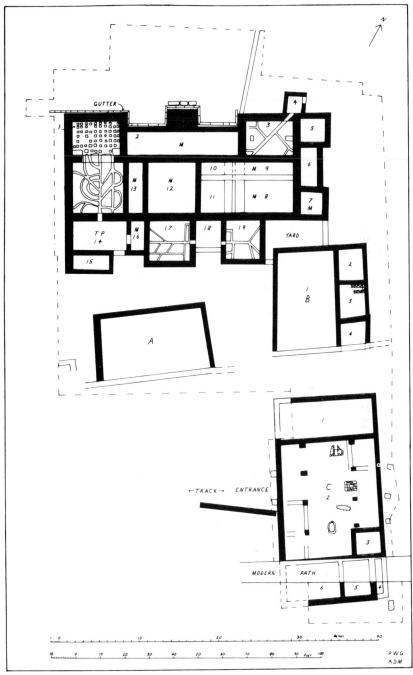

Building XII, 2 found during excavations in Beeches Road, Cirencester, and associated buildings.

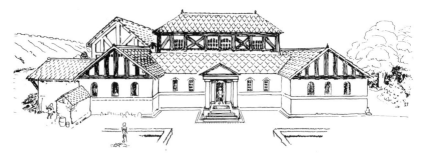

Artist's reconstruction of building XII, 2 found in the Beeches Road.

Underfloor heating in building XII, 2.

black in line with the stokehole. Dating evidence from the building was sparse and not particularly helpful with regard to the structural alterations just described, but they must surely extend into the fifth century A.D. At the north corner of the house stood an outbuilding (XII, 1A) which measured 15m by 8m externally, of which the outside walls were built of stone. There was no sign of an entrance or of any substantial flooring. Many iron nails found within the building may have come from the roof, a raised wooden floor or from some industrial activity. A buttress was needed at the

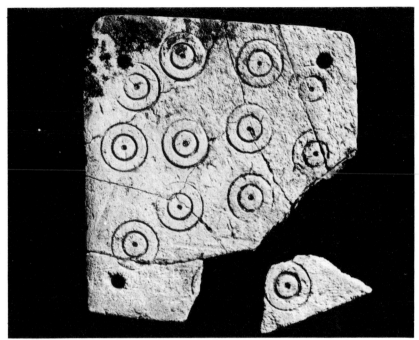

Bone tablet as used in weaving found associated with building XII, 2.

south-east corner, and, with the possibility of a raised floor, the building might have been used to store corn.

To the south was another well-built stone house of fourth-century date (XII, 2) with a series of outbuildings, two of which (A & B) were undoubtedly associated with the main building, whilst the status of the third is uncertain (C). Its plan is striking in that it is similar to that of a winged corridor villa usually to be found at the centre of a farm rather than in a town. In its latest phase it had at least eleven mosaics, eight of which were found *in situ*, although not necessarily complete, and many of the walls were decorated with painted plaster. There were three rooms with channelled hypocausts and one large room or hall with a pillared hypocaust in one half and an elaborate channelled hypocaust in the other. Like the building to the north, various internal alterations and extensions were detected but not always understood. Of considerable interest were the outbuildings. Building XII, 2 A was not examined, but its outline was discernible through the rubble layer beneath the allotment topsoil. However, most of outbuilding XII, 2 B was uncovered and found to consist of one large room with three smaller ones leading off. From unstratified levels, but surely associated with one or other of the buildings excavated, came an iron coulter from a Roman plough and four bone plaques of the sort used in tablet-weaving. Taking into

Aerial view of the Beeches Road site during the course of excavation.

account the plan of the house and the presence of the coulter and the bone tablets, there can be little doubt that we are dealing with a farmhouse and associated sheds or barns built just inside the walls of *Corinium* at some time in the fourth century. Further south another structure was found and shown to be an aisled building with possible living rooms at one end and a store at the other. The discovery of lumps of iron residue and of a probable iron-smithing hearth from inside the aisled part of the building points to it being used in connection with iron-working. It might have been a smithy for the farm to the north or it could have been a small independent farmhouse with store, general workshop area and living quarters. Coins date the use of the building to the late fourth century at the earliest. This remarkable group of houses with their outbuildings was most probably connected with agriculture, perhaps reflecting a move from outside the walls of the town at a time of uncertainty, so that the occupants could live in the security of the town while still continuing to work the land beyond the walls.

3
Large Rural Settlements

Nobody visiting Gloucester or Cirencester during the Roman period, whether native Briton or a Roman from another province, would have been in any doubt about the status of those two settlements. In modern terminology they are best described as cities. There were, however, a group of settlements in Roman Britain which covered as great an area as some cities and possessed a limited number of urban functions but clearly were not cities. Size alone is no criterion as to the status of a settlement. It is necessary to know what buildings existed in order to determine whether it should be called a town, minor town or village. Villages, Professor A.L.F. Rivet argues, were mainly concerned with agriculture and a town with trade, and if sufficient buildings in a settlement have been excavated and identified then it should be possible to classify it as either a town or village. As it happens so little is known about such settlements in Gloucestershire that attempts to classify them need not concern us at present.

Leaving aside single farms or groups of farms, larger settlements are known at Dorn, Bourton-on-the-Water, Lower Slaughter, Dymock, Wycomb, Kingscote, Duntisbourne Rouse and in the region of Lechlade, and there are probably a number of others which are even less-well understood. As already indicated there are an increasing number of sites from lowland Britain whose origins were determined by the presence of the Roman army originally and some of these may fall into this category. Early material has come from Dymock and Kingscote which may reflect the presence of the Roman army initially and the shape and position of Dorn has led several scholars to suggest a military installation in the first instance. From none of these sites, however, is there any firm evidence to support this hypothesis; so for the moment we are still uncertain as to why these settlements should have originated where they did. Once established economic factors are likely to have influenced the way they developed. Not all necessarily owe their position and origin to pre-existing Roman forts. Some may have grown up beside a pre-Roman site or as roadside settlements at convenient points where they could be used by the Public Post or as centres for the collection of the *annona* (corn tax). Let us first of all consider those settlements which lie astride or close to the major Roman roads in the county and begin by investigating those along the Fosse Way.

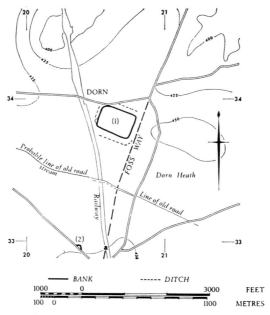

The Roman settlement at Dorn.

DORN

The existence of a site 2km north of Moreton in Marsh has been known since
at least the seventeenth century, but it was not until the area was photographed from the air by Professor J.K.St. Joseph in 1960 that much
attention was paid to the settlement. Since that date a short account of the
excavations conducted by Lt. Col. R.K. Morcom between 1937 and 1939
has appeared. Air photographs and field work revealed a rectangular enclosure
measuring 165m by 248m over the ramparts, an area of about four hectares.
It is surrounded by a ditch 45-60m across with a counterscarp bank beyond.
An inner rampart, now spread by ploughing, was about 30m wide. Inside
the rampart there is the suggestion of a defensive wall and a series of streets
laid out at right angles to each other. The Fosse Way passes close by the
south-east side, almost touching the enclosure.

The excavations of Morcom uncovered a stone building constructed on
what are described as diagonal stone footings, which presumably means
pitched footings, and said to have produced material ranging in date from
the first to the fifth century. The floors were described as being made of
rough stones, but there were some coarse *tesserae* indicating a pavement.
Coloured wall-plaster was also found. Although the building is described by
the excavator and the Royal Commission on Historical Monuments as a

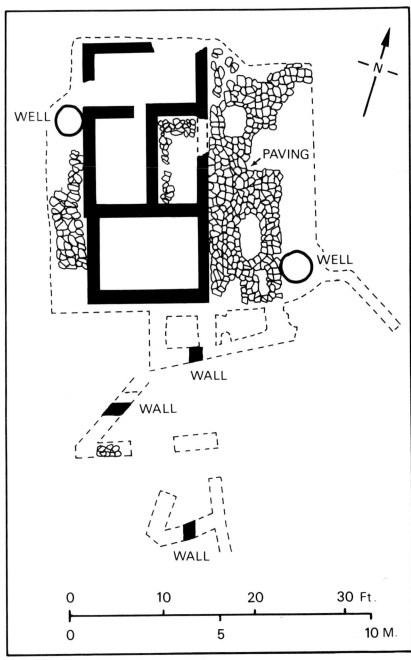

WELL

PAVING

WELL

WALL

WALL

WALL

0   10   20   30 Ft.

0   5   10 M.

Plan of building excavated at Dom, 1937-9.

corridor building, the reason is not apparent. To the east and west, paved surfaces existed which have been variously described as a road or a courtyard, but as there is a well in each area a road seems as unlikely interpretation. There is quite a large collection of pottery from the excavations now housed in Birmingham Museum, the bulk of which, according to Miss V. Rigby, dates from the second half of the second century to the end of the fourth century A.D. However, first-century pottery is present in the form of sherds from six South Gaulish samian vessels and a butt beaker. There is nothing of the same date among the coarse wares, many of which are local and of very similar forms to those found in Cirencester. The most important source of both *mortaria* and colour-coated wares was the Oxfordshire Potteries, and later products of the Nene Valley Potteries found their way to the site. From the excavations also came two steelyards and an ornate spit. Two sculptured stones, possibly altars, were found in the nineteenth century, one of which depicts a *genius*.

Dorn is one of the smallest, if not *the* smallest, settlement to have what appears to be a regular grid-plan of streets. It is also unusual in being situated to one side of the Fosse Way, unlike other settlements along this road. It has been argued by Professor M. Todd that such small settlements could hardly have been wealthy enough to have provided defences out of their own pockets and that these were paid for by central funds because these sites were fulfilling one or more official functions, such as the collection of the *annona*.

BOURTON-ON-THE-WATER AND LOWER SLAUGHTER

Fourteen kilometres south-west of Dorn along the Fosse Way, Roman structures and material have been found over a wide area although not necessarily belonging to a single settlement. Some are in the parish of Bourton-on-the-Water and others in Lower Slaughter.

BOURTON-ON-THE-WATER

Roman finds, including Claudian coins, first- to fourth-century pottery and a possible hut, have been made immediately outside the Salmonsbury Hill Fort. The bulk of the discoveries, however, come from beside the Fosse Way on either side of the River Windrush, covering an area of at least twelve hectares. These include walls, wells, ovens and floors, but no sign of any defences. The so-called 'Leadenwell Villa' at Lansdowne, excavated in 1933-4, was only partly investigated and the plan was incomplete, but of particular interest were two lead tanks capable of holding 181 and 296 litres respectively. Also found were a well and an oven. More substantial remains of an extensive settlement have been found along both sides of the Fosse Way to the north and south of the river Windrush, but mainly concentrated

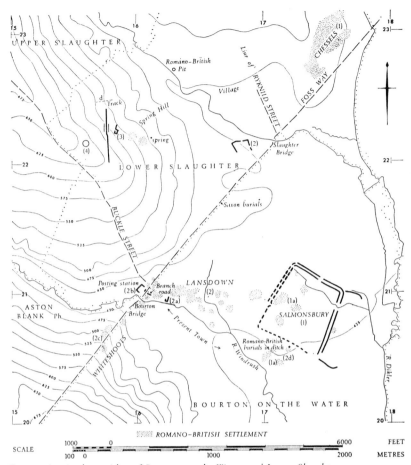

Roman sites in the parishes of Bourton-on-the-Water and Lower Slaughter.

in an area to the north-east of the bridge which carried the road over the river. Roman material has been reported for well over a hundred years, but the most significant exposure of Roman remains was during the construction of the railway from Bourton-on-the-Water to Cheltenham between 1875-81 and its subsequent removal in 1966. In 1958 Bourton Bridge was widened and at various times road works to the north-east of the bridge have uncovered sections of the Fosse Way and roadside buildings. Often working under extremely difficult circumstances, Mrs. H.E. O'Neil has managed to record a great deal about the Roman phase of Bourton's past, sometimes excavating under controlled conditions, and on other occasions rescuing what she could from contractors' trenches. The functions attributed to the

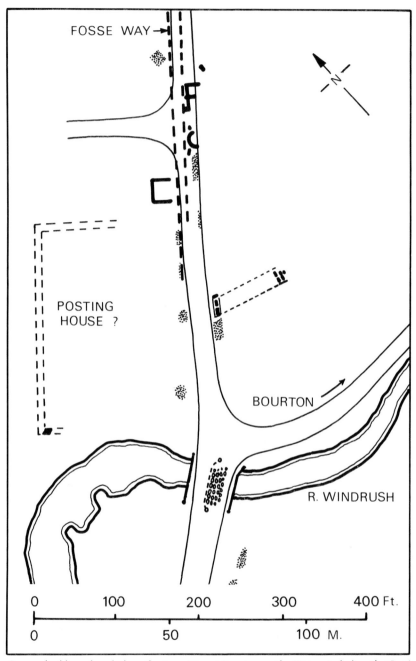

Roman buildings found along the Fosse Way at Bourton-on-the-Water, including the 'Posting House'.

buildings by Mrs O'Neil have been retained although sometimes doubt is cast upon a particular interpretation.

The construction of the railway embankment had revealed a large Roman building which Mrs. O'Neil believes to have been a posting house and when the embankment was finally removed in 1966-7, she excavated a building which may have been a stable attached to it. The stable, a rectangular structure 8.8m by 9.1m built in the late third century, was floored with a mixture of pitched stone, flag-stones and large worn cobbles, suggesting use by animals. An open hearth may have been a forge and another feature an oven. The samples taken from this building contained grasses which were most probably cereals, but they provided no conclusive confirmation of its use as a stable. The absence of a well-constructed drain argues against its use by animals, and the 'narrow runnels between the flags' could hardly have been sufficient for a stable housing several horses. There is a striking similarity between this building and one found outside the Bath Gate at Cirencester, which was involved with a craft using iron.

A possible 'wayside shrine' and 'bakehouse' were found further north on the opposite side of the Fosse Way. The 'shrine', of which only the foundations survived, consisted of two concentric walls 1.5m apart. The walls consisted of one course of well-laid masonry 22-30 cms wide and in the space between was a hard-packed core of small rubble covered by a thin layer of gravel. It is interesting to compare this structure with those found by Mr C. Renfrew south of Bourton Bridge on Whiteshoots Hill. The first, that furthest from Bourton Bridge, was 11m in diameter with only the foundations surviving. A 2m gap in these foundations with a post hole on each side was an entrance which could have accommodated wheeled vehicles and there was an internal wall. The excavator interpreted this building as 'a controlled entrance to the site', but this seems most unlikely and it may, as Mrs. O'Neil suggested for the building she excavated further to the north, have been used for religious purposes. Two other buildings of similar plan excavated by C. Renfrew in the same field could well have had the same function. Next to the 'shrine' found by Mrs. O'Neil was a fourth-century building which, because it contained two ovens, has attracted such names as 'bakehouse' and 'transport cafe'. A well-metalled and cambered street 7.3m wide branched off the Fosse Way between the bridge and the shrine.

The results of excavation and observations at Bourton-on-the-Water have lead several people to postulate that the settlement was a small posting station which provided a range of services for travellers using both the Fosse Way and Ryknild Street, which joins it just to the north. It is not surprising that the local people already living in the area before the conquest were attracted towards this great route which swept across the country and exploited travellers by providing the facilities they required.

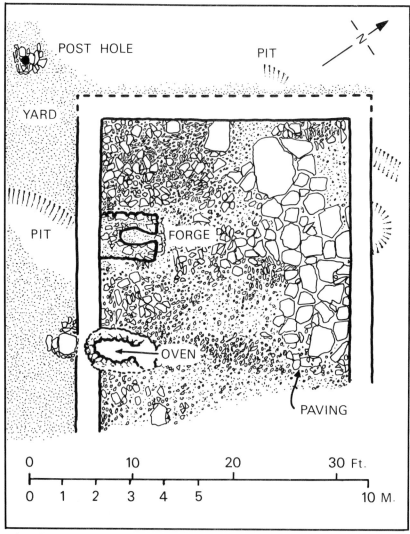

POST HOLE

PIT

YARD

PIT

FORGE

OVEN

PAVING

| 0 | 10 | 20 | 30 Ft. |

| 0 | 1 | 2 | 3 | 4 | 5 | 10 M. |

Plan of 'stables', Bourton-on-the-Water.

LOWER SLAUGHTER

Two and a half kilometres north-east of Bourton Bridge and to one side of the Fosse Way, Roman finds have been made over an area of more than ten hectares in a part of Lower Slaughter known as Chessels. The site, now largely destroyed by quarrying, has benefited from the work of Mrs. H.E. O'Neil and has been shown to consist of many ditches, pits, wells, burials, a

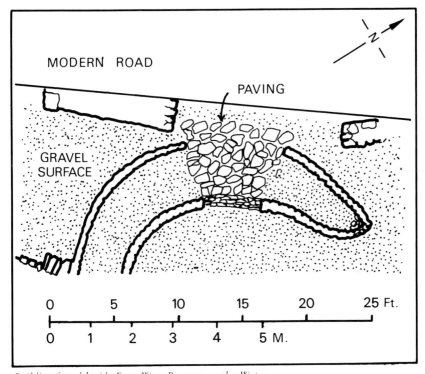

Building found beside Fosse Way, Bourton-on-the-Water.

corn drier and several structures. There is also evidence of pre-Roman occupation.

Two rectangular buildings were apparent (numbers 47 and 67 on plan, page 70) both with areas of pitched-stone paving alongside. From various parts of the site has come an interesting range of objects, a number of which are connected with religious activities. Building 47, built after A.D. 350, was rectangular and divided into six rooms. Fragments of a votive tablet were found nearby and from well 5 came eight votive objects. These include two small uninscribed altars, three votive plaques to Mars and to *Genii Cuculatii*, and two small statuettes of seated headless figures. Other features which have been located in the area include a fourth-century corn drier and two possible forges. The site has the appearance of a native agricultural community, with a possible temple complex, originating in the pre-Roman period and continuing through until the late fourth century.

DYMOCK

This Roman settlement has received very little attention from archaeologists and yet discoveries from the Roman period have been made as far back as

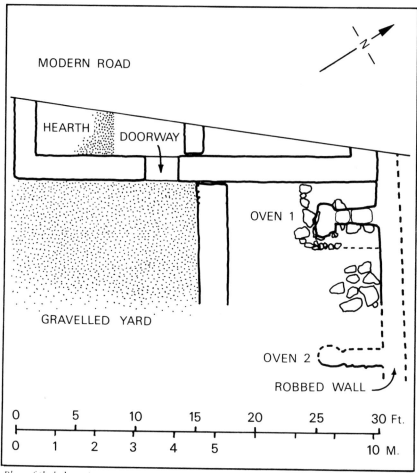

Plan of 'bakehouse' at Bourton-on-the-Water.

1890. The most comprehensive account, written by the Rev. J.E. Gethyn-Jones, relies heavily on the opinion of several archaeologists, whilst a survey of Gloucestershire towns carried out by Dr. R. Leech on behalf of the Committee for Rescue Archaeology in Avon, Gloucester and Somerset has brought together all the printed and unpublished information. Field work since 1958 has been carried out by the Malvern Research Group under P.L. Waters. A Roman road was photographed from the air by A. Baker in 1958 and was visible as an agger west of Crowfield Farm. It was sectioned in 1959 and noted in various places over the years, in particular to the east of Crowfield Farm when the M50 was under construction. Previously un-

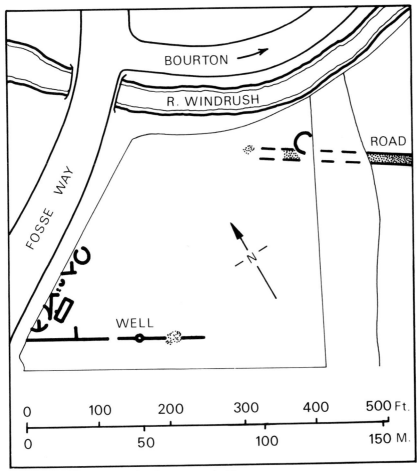

Buildings recently uncovered at Bourton-on-the-Water.

recorded, it perhaps linked the settlement at Dymock with one at Oldbury, Tewkesbury. The road from Gloucester to the south joins this road within the area where Roman finds have been made.

Excavations by the Malvern Research Group have revealed a series of foundations and floors of both stone and timber buildings. Material ranges in date from the Claudian period to the third century with an apparent absence of the fourth-century coins and pottery so frequently found on most Roman sites. At least one *Dobunnic* coin has come from Dymock. During excavations carried out near the cricket pitch between 1960 and 1966 evidence of iron smelting, two possible bowl furnaces and three early

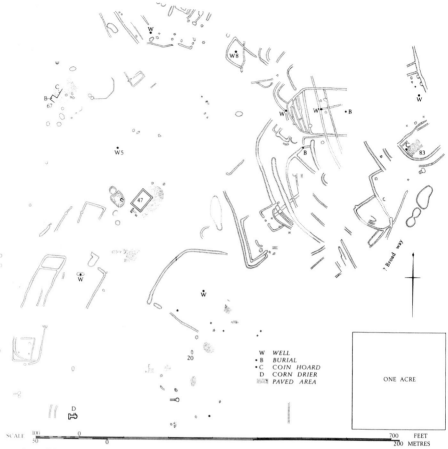

Plan of features found at Lower Slaughter.

parallel ditches were found. In the Ravenna Cosmography, a list of countries, towns and rivers of the Roman world compiled by a late seventh-century unknown cleric, two settlements are recorded on the road between Gloucester and Kenchester. One is probably at Stretton Grandison whilst the other, possibly Dymock, is listed as *Macatonion* (or *Magalonium*).

WYCOMB

The existence of a large Roman settlement at Wycomb, in the parishes of Andoversford and Whittington, has been well known since excavations were conducted there in 1863-1864 by W.L. Lawrence. Prehistoric finds from the Mesolithic period to the Iron Age are known and from this latter period

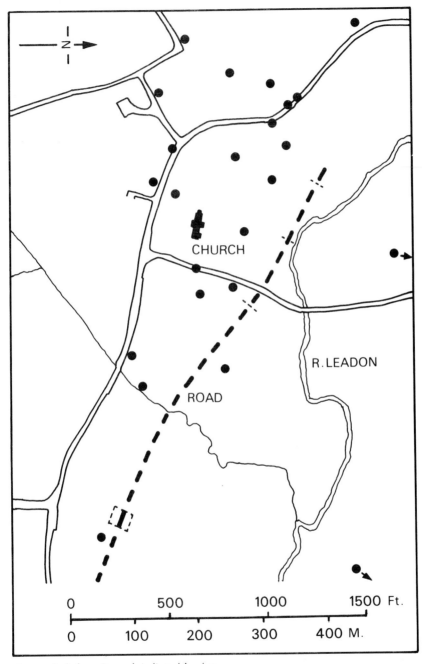

Roman finds from Dymock indicated by dots.

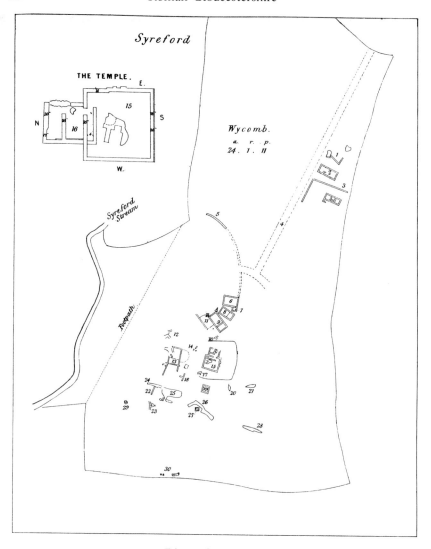

WYCOMB
PLAN BY W. L. LAWRENCE 1864

come three *Dobunnic* coins, one of which is inscribed EISU. Aerial photographs and excavation indicate that the Roman settlement extended over an area of at least eleven hectares on flat ground to the east of the river Coln and contained paved streets and stone buildings, but so far no trace of any defensive circuit is known. However, a ditch with a rounded bottom, 6m across and 1.2m deep, was excavated between Black Close and the railway embankment and one wonders whether this could be part of such a system. A major street runs through the settlement from the north-east to the south-west with a number of side streets at right angles to it. It then joins another significant road apparently under the railway embankment. When Lawrence examined the main thoroughfare he found it to be 2.4-3m wide and to comprise large stones set vertically and smaller stones laid flat.

A series of buildings is drawn on the plan accompanying Lawrence's excavation report, containing 'hypocausts, pavements, forges and fireplaces'. Building No. 15, which measured 12.5m square internally, is interpreted as a Romano-Celtic temple which appears to have been built over a smaller two-roomed structure (16). A 23m isolated stretch of wall (5) has been drawn on Lawrence's plan as a continuous curve, suggesting to some people that it was part of a theatre wall. There is no clear indication why the wall is shown as continuous and the interpretation as part of a theatre must remain conjectural. However, attention has been drawn by Professor S.S. Frere to the frequent association of temple and theatre, and the idea of a theatre at Wycomb is plausible. Some simple rectangular buildings, very sketchy in outline, (6, 8, 9) have the appearance of shops. As from other large settlements in Gloucestershire, there is an interesting group of finds from Wycomb including a group of votive objects, one of which portrays a *genius cucullatus* and two hoodless deities. Coins and pottery more or less cover the whole Roman period in date and there is an interesting range of iron tools from the site.

KINGSCOTE

Eighteen kilometres west-south-west of Cirencester and south of Ashel Barn in an area known as The Chessalls lies an extensive Roman settlement covering at least seven fields and measuring approximately thirty hectares. Recent work by the Kingscote Archaeological Association under the direction of E.J. Swain and M. Parris has contributed a great deal to our understanding of this extremely significant site, and for this reason it is probably the best-known site of its type in Gloucestershire. In some ways it bears comparison with other such settlements from the county in having paved roads and a sizeable area of buildings and in being undefended, but there are some noticeable differences, particularly in the quality of the finds which have come from Kingscote. It may seem strange for a settlement of this size not to be situated on one of the known major roads but, as we know so

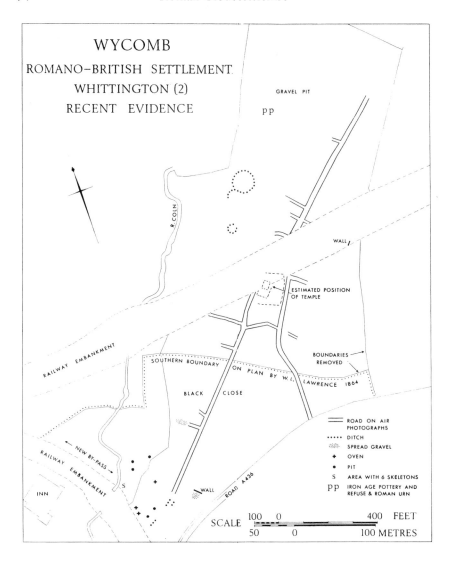

WYCOMB

ROMANO–BRITISH SETTLEMENT
WHITTINGTON (2)
RECENT EVIDENCE

GRAVEL PIT

pp

R. COLN

WALL

ESTIMATED POSITION
OF TEMPLE

BOUNDARIES
REMOVED

RAILWAY EMBANKMENT

SOUTHERN BOUNDARY ON PLAN BY W.L. LAWRENCE 1864

BLACK CLOSE

ROAD ON AIR
PHOTOGRAPHS
DITCH
SPREAD GRAVEL
OVEN
PIT
S   AREA WITH 6 SKELETONS
pp   IRON AGE POTTERY AND
     REFUSE & ROMAN URN

NEW BY-PASS
RAILWAY EMBANKMENT

INN

S

WALL

ROAD A436

SCALE   100   0   400   FEET

50   0   100 METRES

little about the dozens of minor roads that existed, its position may not be so unusual.

The excavations between 1975-1980 have concentrated on a building to the north-west of the occupied area in a field known as Middle Chessalls. Here a house and associated outbuildings have been uncovered and their development studied in detail. The conclusions drawn from these particular

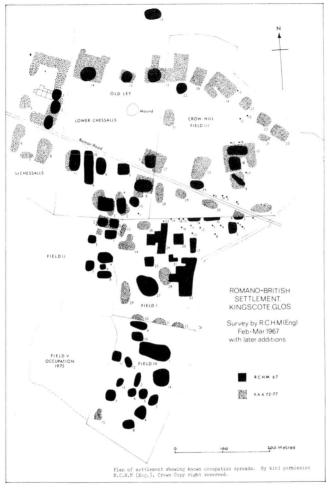

ROMANO-BRITISH
SETTLEMENT.
KINGSCOTE.GLOS

Survey by R C H M (Eng)
Feb-Mar 1967
with later additions

■ R C H M 67

▨ K A A 72-77

0   100   200 Metres

Plan of settlement showing known occupation spreads. By kind permission
R.C.H.M (Eng.), Crown Copy right reserved.

Extent of Roman building debris found in the plough soil at Kingscote.

investigations must be treated with caution and not necessarily applied to the
whole settlement, as the area so far opened up only represents less than one
per cent of the area covered by Roman buildings, a very small sample upon
which to draw conclusions.

The earliest sign of activity on the site consisted of a series of large pits dug
into the natural subsoil to obtain stone. These quarry pits were backfilled
with material which points to them having been dug around the middle of
the second century A.D. Eventually, in the early part of the third century,
stone buildings with dry-stone walls were erected. These were rectangular

Aerial Photograph by Dr. Colin Pennycuick.

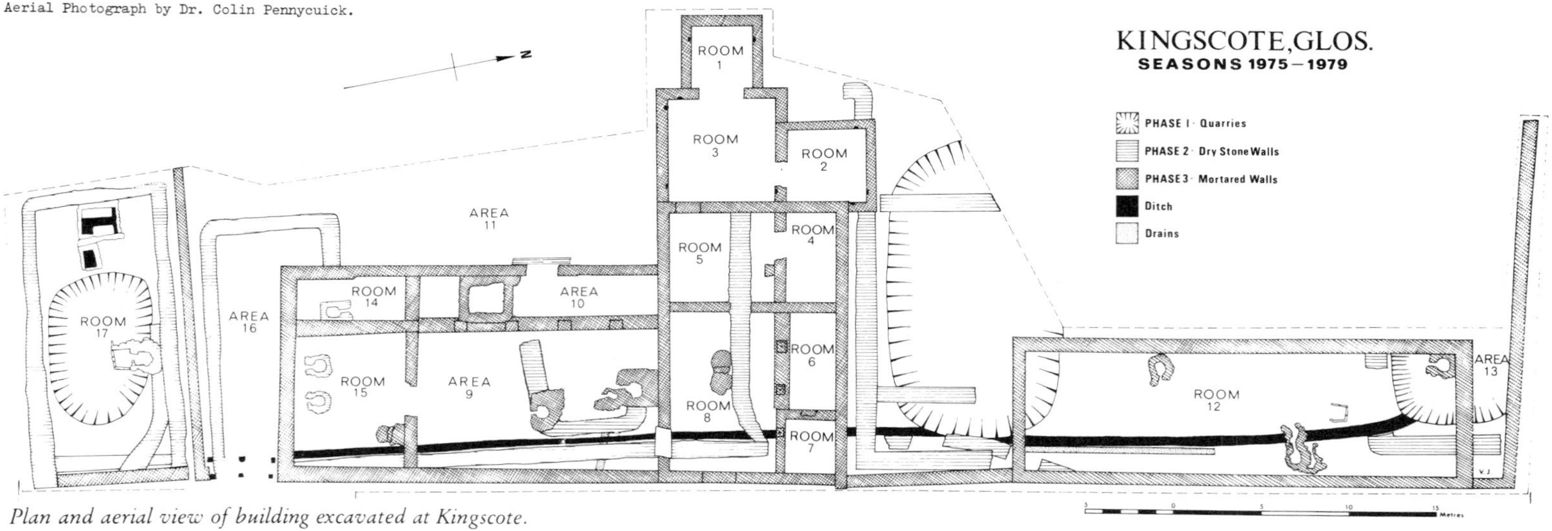
KINGSCOTE, GLOS.
SEASONS 1975–1979
PHASE 1 · Quarries
PHASE 2 · Dry Stone Walls
PHASE 3 · Mortared Walls
Ditch
Drains
N
ROOM 1
ROOM 2
ROOM 3
ROOM 4
ROOM 5
ROOM 6
ROOM 7
ROOM 8
AREA 9
AREA 10
AREA 11
ROOM 12
AREA 13
ROOM 14
ROOM 15
AREA 16
ROOM 17
5 0 5 10 15 Metres

Plan and aerial view of building excavated at Kingscote.

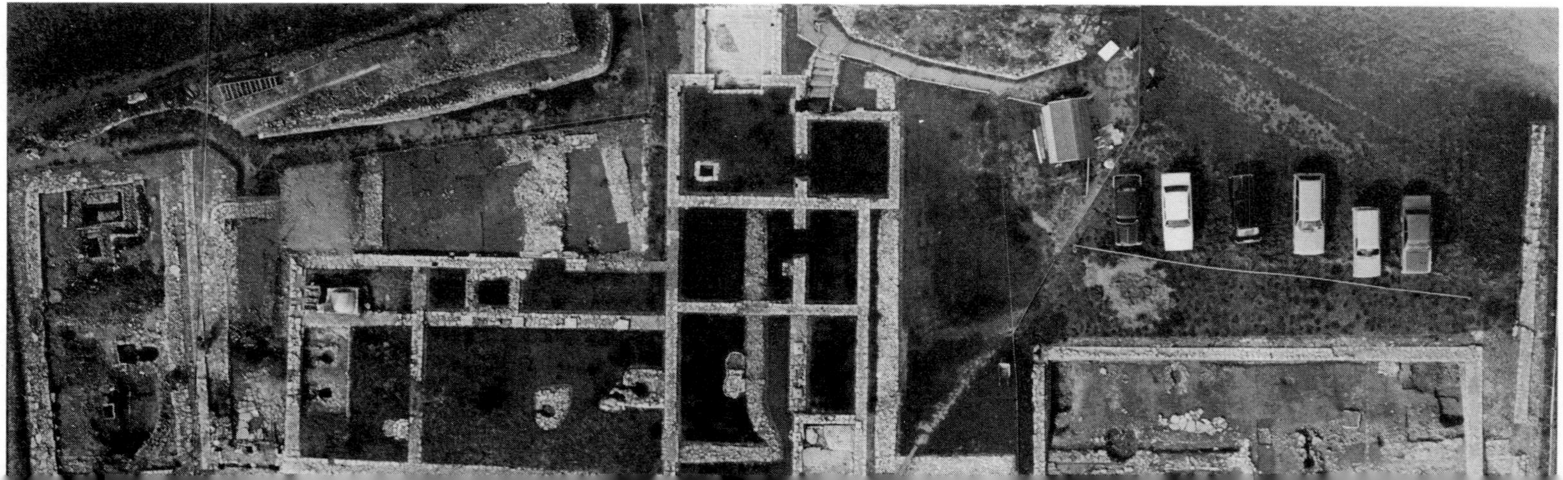

and had rounded corners and they continued to be used until the closing years of the third century when a house with well-appointed rooms was built. Outbuildings were later added to the north and south and the whole complex was enclosed within a stone wall with at least one timber gateway. Room 1 contained a mosaic floor which has been lifted and is on display in the Corinium Museum, Cirencester. The design consists of a central medallion containing a female bust facing the entrance to the room and, assuming the oval object above the left shoulder to be a mirror, then it seems most likely that this is a representation of Venus. The entrance from room 3 into room 1 is paved with an aquatic scene depicting two dolphins. Both mosaics are dated to the fourth century. The walls of room 1 were also decorated with attractively-painted plaster and a great deal of this which had fallen from the walls was found during excavation, carefully lifted and restored with the help of Dr. N. Davey; it is on permanent loan to the Corinium Museum. According to Professor J.M.C. Toynbee, the painting represents Achilles disguised as a woman in the Court of Lykomedes on the Island of Skyros. Room 2 also contained a mosaic floor and its walls were painted, although insufficient of either remained to reconstruct it in any detail. There was evidence from room 5 to suggest that it was destroyed by fire causing the roof to collapse and its tiles to fall, where they remained until uncovered by the excavators. Details of the roof construction also came from room 8 where many tiles were found, all of which were made from sandstone and fashioned in the usual diamond shape, graduating in size, with small tiles at the ridge and the largest ones at the eaves. Ridge tiles were found in several rooms and in room 8 two fragments of a limestone roof finial were also recovered. Room 7 seems to have served a specific purpose as it was provided with a substantial floor made of large stone slabs, and had a drain. The excavators believe it was used for some industrial purpose involving water.

Some idea of the occupation upon which those living in this building might have been engaged comes from an outbuilding at the north-east corner of the site. Here stood a barn-like building, measuring 22.7m by 6.7m, with a large entrance in the centre of the east wall and a cobbled yard outside. Inside were found 'four key-hole-shaped ovens', a square raised platform identified as a brazier stand and a timber drain in the southern half of the building. During the course of excavation a considerable quantity of decorated bone inlay and bronze terminals was found, which may have been used in making furniture. To the south of this group of buildings was a rectangular dry-stone-walled building in which there was a T-shaped corn-drying oven and one or two other areas where there were ovens or hearths. Two large mill-stones were also recovered from this building, each having a diameter of about 80cms. Several possible tracks exist in the area of the buildings and one road has been investigated and shown to have been 9m

Mosaic excavated at Kingscote.

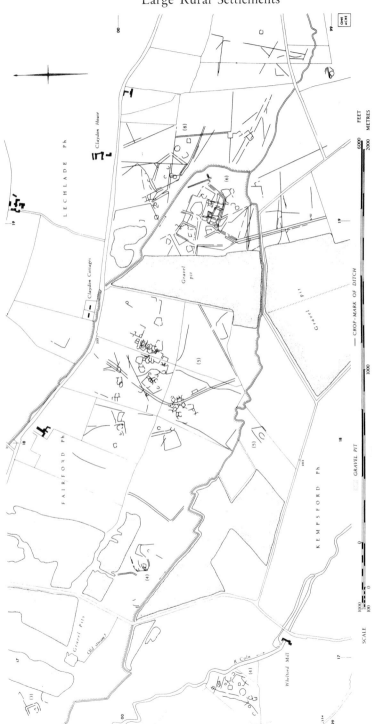

ONE
ACRE

FEET
METRES

6000

2000

LECHLADE Ph

Claydon House

Claydon Cottages

Gravel
Pit

Gravel
Pit

FAIRFORD Ph

CROP-MARK OF DITCH

Gravel Pits

Old stream?

GRAVEL PIT

KEMPSFORD Ph

R. Coln

Whelford Mill

SCALE

1000   0

100   0

Settlements, tracks and enclosures as revealed by aerial photography in the Fairford/Lechlade area.

wide with side ditches 60-90cms deep and to have been paved. Roads leading to and from the settlement must have existed, as well as a reasonably well-made road linking it with Cirencester, either direct or via the Fosse Way. Two roads in the vicinity of Kingscote have been tentatively identified as being Roman although their alignment is often uncertain.

LECHLADE/FAIRFORD

An extensive area of crop marks in the Thames valley on the south borders of the county reflects a maze of mainly ditches and tracks which have the appearance of being connected with continuous independent agricultural communities, settled cheek by jowl on the fertile and productive soils of the river valley. It seems unlikely that they had any communal organisation such as there was at Kingscote or Wycomb. Here in the parishes of Fairford and Lechlade several hundred hectares show indications of land usage in the Roman period, but so far nothing has been found which might indicate anything approaching an urban status.

****

There are other settlements in the county which cover more than four hectares, but very few details are known of them other than those afforded by field walking or by a study of surviving earth-works. One such site can be seen at Duntisbourne Rouse 6.4km north-west of Cirencester and there are others at Ampney Crucis, Baunton, Coberley, Down Ampney, Elkstone and Sherborne to name but a few. Although some may have been associated with a particular industrial activity the majority, like most of the larger settlements discussed in this chapter, were agricultural communities.

4
Agriculture

Agriculture in Roman Britain, as Professor Frere wrote some years ago, must be considered on two levels. First there are the peasant settlements, whether villages or simple farmsteads, which are to be seen as a continuation of the pre-Roman pattern and appear to have been little affected by Roman rule as far as their buildings were concerned. Slowly they began to use Roman-style pottery and coins, but not in large quantities. Such settlements rarely contained materials in their buildings which could be noticed on the ground by the casual observer and so it is only in recent years, with increased field walking and aerial photography, that such sites have been recognised and seen to be a significant part of the rural landscape. However, although our knowledge of peasant farms is meagre and indeed a detailed study of them is long overdue, as more are discovered and plotted on to maps it become increasingly clear that the pattern of agricultural exploitation in the Roman period was one of intensive farming over much of the county, thus continuing a tradition which is now recognised as having existed long before the Roman occupation.

At the other end of the scale there are the rural houses, built in Roman style and generally expressing a high level of culture and comfort. Most of the information about farms comes from the many such buildings found over the past two to three hundred years, the majority of which are to be found in lowland Britain. These villas, as they were known, were an independent economic unit and the main house usually contained heated rooms or baths, mosaic floors and decorated wall-plaster and had sophisticated architectural features, such as columns. As they were built in stone, their remains have been frequently noted by past generations of antiquarians, and the discovery of mosaic floors has aroused much local interest, especially among wealthy landowners on whose property villas were often found. Occasionally these interested amateurs commissioned excavations and had the remains preserved, and, when mosaics were discovered, had accurate drawings made or even arranged for them to be lifted and displayed in a museum or country house. It should be stated at this point that not all the romanised buildings in the countryside which had mosaics and hypocausts were necessarily concerned with agriculture or horticulture. Some may have been connected with industries such as pottery-making, stone

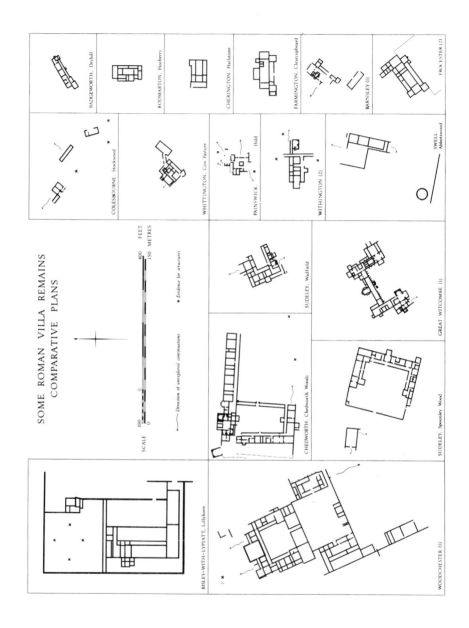

SOME ROMAN VILLA REMAINS
COMPARATIVE PLANS

SCALE

100   0
0   150 METRES
400 FEET

✗ *Evidence for structures*

Direction of unexplored continuations

BADGEWORTH, Dryhill

RODMARTON, Hocberry

CHERINGTON, Hailstone

FARMINGTON, Clearcupboard

BARNSLEY (I)

FROCESTER (2)

COLESBOURNE, Stockwood

WHITTINGTON, Cow Pasture

PAINSWICK, Ifold

WITHINGTON (2)

SWELL, Abbotswood

SUDELEY, Watfield

CHEDWORTH, Chedworth Woods

GREAT WITCOMBE (I)

SUDELEY, Spoonley Wood

BISLEY-WITH-LYPIATT, Lillyhorn

WOODCHESTER (I)

extraction or mining, or with a religious establishment; clearly some were the homes of the rich and influential, as must be the case with the Woodchester palace, as perhaps it should be called.

There are around 45-50 villas in Gloucestershire and this number is certain to grow as more intensive field work is undertaken, and when such work already undertaken is published. As the sample grows, more reliability can be placed on their spatial distribution within the county, and the reasons for it may be formulated. The majority of those sites listed as villas by the Royal Commission on Historical Monuments and the Ordnance Survey lie in the Cotswolds. This figure might well be different had the Commission carried out a similar survey in the Vale and Forest, but even so it seems clear that the majority of villas were in the Cotswolds. Field work on the line of the M5 motorway in Gloucestershire and neighbouring counties has shown extensive Roman settlement along the line of the Roman road between Sea Mills and Gloucester, but only two sites which may have been villas, at Upton St Leonards and Brookthorpe Court. Many of the sites seem to date from the second half of the first century A.D. when the area must have been deliberately cleared of trees for settlement. If the sample revealed on the M5 is representative of the whole area between the Cotswolds and the River Severn, then there are about 4,500 Romano-British sites in the Vale of which 4,400 await discovery! The same story may be repeated on the other side of the River Severn in the Forest of Dean, where villas have been found close to the river at Aylburton, Boughspring and Woolaston, but there we have no evidence of the kind provided by the M5 field work to indicate whether or not there was extensive native settlement. Further into the heartland of the Forest there are no villas that have been recorded, and our knowledge of settlement in that area is meagre.

Thanks to the meticulous work of a number of excavators, a great deal has been learnt in the past decade about the origins and development of several villas in the county. The most recently-excavated examples are at Barnsley Park, Farmington and Frocester Court, whilst selective trenching at Chedworth and a reappraisal of the architecture of Great Witcombe have helped in understanding earlier work on those two sites.

The villa at FROCESTER is typical of an average-sized farm, and, thanks to the work of E.G. Price and the late Capt. H.S. Gracie, we have learnt much about its buildings and economy. The farmhouse, built about A.D. 275, stood in a compound demarcated by ditches and had massive foundations, perhaps indicating an upper storey. It consisted of a rectangular block 32m long and 10m wide divided internally into a large central hall (2) with a smaller room on either side, one of which was separated from the large room by a passageway. The hall was partitioned into three parts each with a floor of different material, and in the south-west corner was an oven and a soakaway, pointing to its use as a kitchen. A heavily-burnt oval-shaped area in

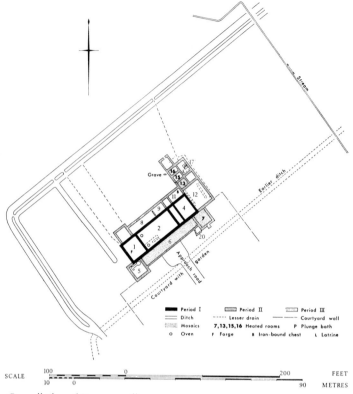

Overall plan of Frocester villa.

room 1 was associated with many nails, pieces of iron, and iron and copper slag, suggesting that it was a forge. Crucibles and fragments of clipped bronze show that bronze was also being worked as well as iron. The narrow passageway between rooms 2 and 4 could have accommodated the stairs for the upper storey. Room 4 had an *opus signinum* floor and quarter-round moulding at the junction of wall and floor. Two groups of minute *tesserae* from the robber trenches surrounding this room may have come from a wall mosaic rather than a floor, although such mosaics were extremely rare in Roman Britain.

Shortly after A.D. 275 a front corridor with projecting rooms at either end was added, along with a row of small rooms at the back of the house. Four pillar bases to the north-east of the original block were probably part of an open-sided shed and room 5 eventually contained a corn drier. The corridor, although originally flagged, was provided with a mosaic in the fourth century and room 7 had a hypocaust inserted, probably at the same

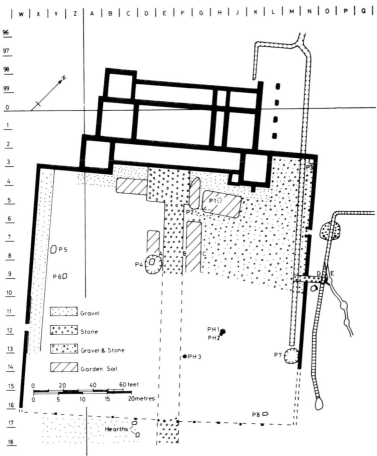

Features in the courtyard of the Frocester villa at the beginning of the fourth century A.D.

time as the floor was changed in the corridor. An unusual find was made in room 11, where sunk into the floor were the remains of an iron-bound chest, presumably a strong box. Various alterations took place during the life of the farm house, the last significant alteration involving the removal of the open-sided shed and the addition of a bath suite, some time around A.D. 360.

In front of the house was a courtyard built towards the end of the third century, in which there were formal garden beds on either side of an approach road. The north-east and south-west sides of the courtyard were marked by a dry-stone wall with a gate in each side; the south-east side, however, consisted only of a wooden fence with a gate across the road. There may have been a fence around the entire courtyard originally, two

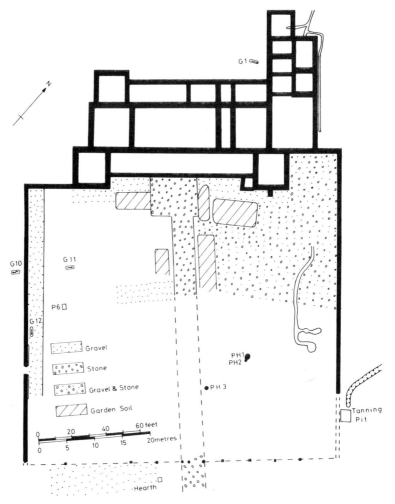

The courtyard of the Frocester villa at the end of the fourth century A.D.

sides of which were later replaced with a wall. The road, which was cambered and 4m wide in its final phase, was edged with kerb stones and had a turning area immediately in front of the house. Alongside the road and in front of the house were a hedge and garden beds which were dug into the stone and gravel of the courtyard and filled with dark loam. Because of the pot sherds, broken bones, jewellery and hairpins found in this loam, the excavators concluded that the beds had been manured with compost from the kitchen refuse dump and that the 'ladies took an interest in the flowers'!

An artist's reconstruction of the Frocester villa.

Through a gate in the north-east wall of the courtyard was a dipping pool, an elaborately-flushed latrine and a possible collecting point for drinking-water. When the bath suite was added to the house in the fourth century the latrine was transfered there, and at about the same time a tanning pit was dug outside the courtyard. The excavators also think that they found evidence for a dovecot and an orchard or shrubbery.

The meticulous care taken with the excavation means that over five thousand animal bones were recovered, enabling a picture of animal husbandry on the farm to be built up. Beef was always the most important meat and its use increased here during the Roman period whilst mutton became less popular. Other bones found on the site show the presence of goat, pig, horse, dog, red deer, roe deer, cat, fox, vole and hare. The presence of bird bones in household rubbish indicates an increase in the use of birds as food, with domestic fowl accounting for the largest group. Other bird bones identified include quail, teal, kite, curlew, skylark, thrush, buzzard, mallard, goose, dove, rook or crow, jackdaw and robin, although not all were necessarily eaten. Other aspects of life on the farm are revealed from the samples of grain, which on analysis were shown to include barley, wheat and seeds of weed grasses. Charcoal samples showed the presence of oak, ash, poplar, hawthorn, box and hazel. The villa's owners also had a taste for oysters, mussels and whelks.

Excavations in 1980 discovered a late first-century well from which came a great deal of organic material. It was 5.5m deep and 58cms in diameter and constructed within a 2.8m circular shaft. Finds include traces of two wooden buckets, a wooden-handled knife and various leather shoes. There were also hazelnuts and walnuts in the fill of the well along with evidence of many animals including ox, sheep, goat, water vole, hedgehog, frog and toad.

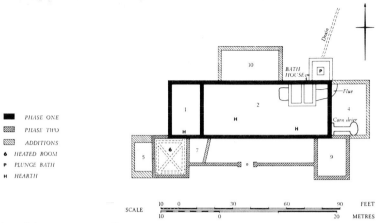

PHASE ONE
PHASE TWO
ADDITIONS
6 *HEATED ROOM*
P *PLUNGE BATH*
H *HEARTH*

Plan of the Farmington villa.

Just over a kilometre to the north-east of Northleach and 500m south-east of the Fosse Way is the site of a villa, the development of which shows certain similarities with Frocester. It lies in the parish of FARMINGTON and is sometimes known as CLEARCUPBOARD. Again the villa began as a simple rectangular block, on this occasion measuring 28m by 9.5m, but divided into only two areas, the largest of which, almost certainly a hall, was some 6m longer than the large central hall at Frocester. It contained numerous hearths, fire pits and a variety of flooring materials and, according to the excavators, may have been roofed, if not entirely, at least in part. The initial building work probably started some time during the first half of the fourth century. The addition of a front corridor and projecting rooms is again analogous with Frocester, as is the later insertion of a channelled hypocaust into one of these rooms. The latest detectable building alterations were the addition of rooms 4, 5 and 10, one of which (4) contained a corn drier. At some stage during the life of the house a small bath suite was inserted into the north-east corner of the central hall (2) with a cold plunge bath situated outside the north wall. Some rooms had painted plaster on their walls, but there was no evidence of any mosaic floors. The roof was covered with stone tiles with tapering ridging stones. A box-flue-tile was stamped before firing with the letters VLA (see chapter 5). The animal bones recovered from the site included those from pig, sheep and cow and analysis of the charcoal from the stokehole to the bath suite revealed samples of ash, birch, hazel and possibly hawthorn or elder. By comparison, it is interesting to note that coal was frequently encountered at Frocester. None of the fifth- or sixth-century grass-tempered pottery found at Frocester has been found at Farmington, and the latest coin is dated to A.D. 350, which points to the absence of late fourth- or fifth-century occupation.

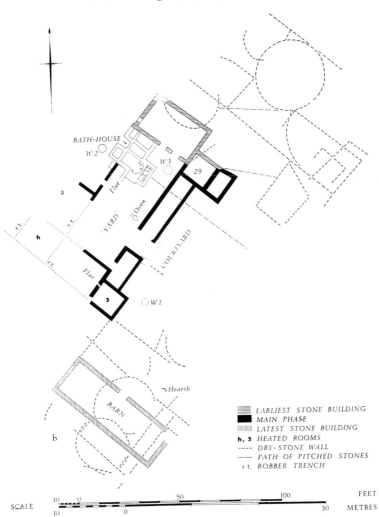

Overall plan of the Barnsley Park villa.

Five kilometres north-east of Cirencester in the grounds of BARNSLEY PARK is an extensive Roman field system associated with a group of farm buildings which provide interesting points of comparison with both Farmington and Frocester. The earliest signs of activity in the area are a series of gullies, post-holes and hearths which probably belonged to a timber building of late second-century date, of which there is little trace apart from a small stone bath-house which was later incorporated into the main farmhouse. Two circular cattle-pens at the southern end of the site, dating from about A.D. 280-330, were replaced by a barn which continued in use

D

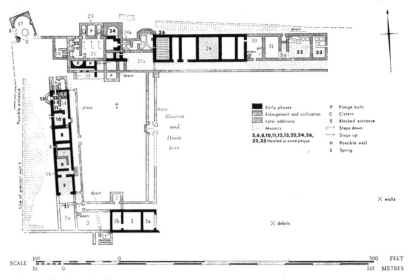

Plan of Chedworth villa.

until after A.D. 380, as did the latest courtyard surface between the barn and house, where ruts testify to fairly extensive use after that date. The main block dates to after *c.* A.D. 360 and, following major modifications, including an extension to the south wing, was converted into agricultural use, possibly as a yard, before finally becoming the base for a timber building or a haystack. The final phases of the villa are obscure. The absence of coins after those issued under the House of Valentinian indicates that there was no activity on the farm after the late fourth century. However, the discovery of fifth-century grass-tempered pottery in the fields shows that the land was still being cultivated, but probably not from the same farmhouse as before. Of the objects recovered from the excavations it is particularly interesting to note the twenty-seven *styli*, twenty-three oxgoads and 910 coins. Dr. Webster believes that these finds indicate the presence of drovers who were employed to drive sheep and cattle to the Cirencester market, and that the site was a collecting point for animals from a larger estate.

No account of Roman villas in Gloucestershire would be complete without CHEDWORTH, the only villa in the county open for public viewing. After its accidental discovery in 1864 the landowner, the Earl of Eldon, paid for the remains to be uncovered and for a museum to house the objects. The National Trust bought the site in 1924 and remain the owners to this day. The most significant advances in the understanding of the history of Chedworth came from small selective excavations carried out by Professor

Sir Ian Richmond between 1958 and 1965. Since then R. Goodburn has undertaken some further exploratory work and has been responsible for writing the most comprehensive survey of the villa to appear in print.

The site is at the head of a small valley, close to a continuous supply of water and protected by the surrounding valley slopes. The conifers, which dominate the landscape today, are a recent introduction and during the villa's life the tree cover was probably less dense and of the deciduous variety. The builders, having once selected this particular spot, had to contend with the steepness of the valley sides and built their foundations on a series of level platforms so that, when completed, the architecture of the villa reflected these different levels. To begin with there were three separate blocks on the north, west and south sides of the valley respectively, erected during the first half of the second century. There are few signs of luxury at this stage and the buildings had a utilitarian look about them. The west block seems to have been the main house and there was a small bath suite in the north range. A water cistern lay to the north-west. The west and south ranges were rebuilt in the late second century after a fire, and at the same time the baths in the north block were enlarged and several rooms were added. It was in the early fourth century that these separate blocks were brought into a unified scheme with the creation of the garden court and the provision of verandahs linking the rooms and the individual blocks. The dining room (5) was now enlarged and baths of the Turkish variety, involving the circulation of steam, were installed in the same range. By contrast the baths in the north range were converted into Swedish or sauna baths. Water which supplied the villa came from a spring beyond the north-west corner of the buildings and fed a reservoir. In the early fourth century this water was led into an octagonal basin capable of holding 4,700 litres within an apsidal building, most likely a shrine to a water-goddess. Around A.D. 370 extensive alterations took place, mainly internal and involving the laying of at least eight mosaic floors.

The site museum gives an idea of the objects which have come from the villa and from other buildings in the neighbourhood. The availability of local limestone meant that many objects of stone were made and have survived. There are altars, pieces of sculpture and architectural features such as columns, roof finials and balustrades. However, not all the stone used in the villa was local; imported white marble was used to cover wall surfaces, Millstone Grit for querns, and sandstone occasionally as a roof covering. Iron tools include part of a spade, a mattock plough, a saw and a pair of shears, giving some indication of the agricultural activities in which the owners of this villa were engaged. Perhaps the largest objects to have come from the forges of Romano-British smiths are the iron beams used to support the boiler, which was situated above the furnace and provided steam and hot water for the baths. Three examples have been found at Chedworth,

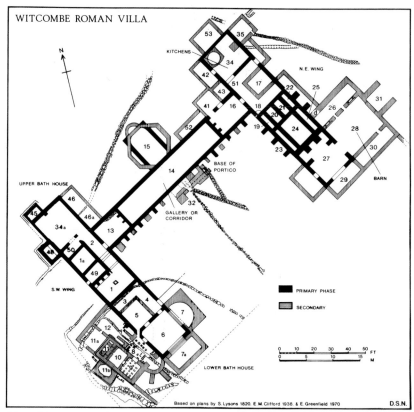

WITCOMBE ROMAN VILLA

KITCHENS

N.E. WING

BASE OF PORTICO

UPPER BATH HOUSE

GALLERY OR CORRIDOR

S.W. WING

BARN

PRIMARY PHASE

SECONDARY

LOWER BATH HOUSE

Based on plans by S.Lysons 1820, E.M.Clifford 1938, & E.Greenfield 1970   D.S.N.

Plan of Great Witcombe villa.

the heaviest of which weighs 219kg and was probably made from iron extracted in the Forest of Dean. The usual range of bronze objects has been recovered from the villa and there is a suggestion that bronze was being made and worked at Chedworth. A crucible has been shown by scientific analysis to have been used to produce a bronze alloy. Coins and pottery show that the farm was very much alive in the latter part of fourth century, as one third of all the coins date to the House of Valentinian (A.D. 364-383).

Another villa which utilised the slope of the ground to bring out architectural features was at GREAT WITCOMBE. Here the designers had to contend with several springs which tended to make the ground wet and unstable, and eventually they produced a plan which had some very unusual features. The major part of the building dates from about A.D. 250 and consists of two blocks linked by a corridor, or 'gallery' as it has become known. On the north-west side of the gallery, in its final stage, was an octagonal room with

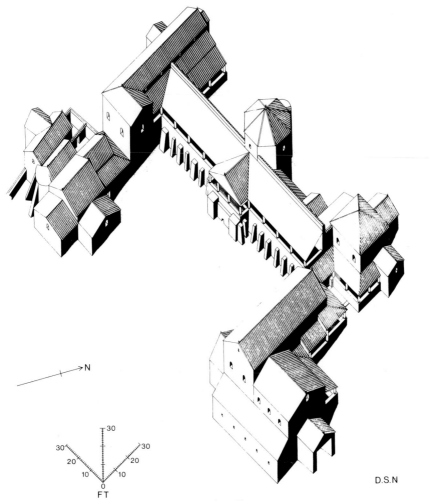

N

30
30   30
20   20
10   10
0
FT

D.S.N

A suggested reconstruction of the Great Witcombe villa.

an attached apse which may have been a shrine. The gallery was heavily buttressed on the downhill side and there were other walls which were reinforced in this way, some of which probably rose to a second floor. The north-east block contained no mosaics and one room is interpreted as a kitchen, which points to the use of this area as service quarters for the villa. The main feature of the south-west wing was the bath suite, several rooms of which had fine mosaics. Differences in floor levels within the villa are clearly reflected in the steps, for example between rooms 1 and 34a, and in a recent reassessment of the villa D.S. Neal shows how, by postulating a second story in several places, the whole of the villa plan becomes intelligible.

So far the villas discussed range from simple cottages, perhaps later extended into winged corridor villas such as at Frocester and Farmington, to more elaborate courtyard villas such as at Chedworth, or the individual design at Great Witcombe with its special architectural features. In a category of its own, however, is WOODCHESTER. Here one is reminded of the so-called palace at Fishbourne, and certainly, from what is known so far, Woodchester bears comparison with that building. Our knowledge of the site comes in the main from the 1793-6 excavations of Samuel Lysons when he uncovered sixty-four rooms arranged around three courts covering in all about one hectare. The centrepiece of this magnificent building was the room on the furthest side from the entrance of court A — the inner sanctum. This room or hall contained the now famous Orpheus mosaic pavement which still lies buried in the ground and is occasionally opened for public viewing. A replica of this floor has been made and is on view in Wotton-under-Edge. It is 15.2m square with a central square of 7.6m containing concentric circles of animals and birds. At each corner of the square was a column, perhaps to support a dome. This, along with the circular mosaic pattern of the floor, formed a unified architectural scheme. One and a half million tesserae were needed to lay the Orpheus mosaic, and, taking into account all the other mosaics found at Woodchester, this must have been one of the biggest contracts ever won by the firm of mosaicists employed there.

The fourth-century plan of the villa has the appearance of a single creation rather than a collection of buildings which had evolved over two to three centuries. Here and there, however, are signs of what might be earlier walls, and the presence of quantities of second-century samian pottery points to earlier occupation on the site. It is just possible that the part of the villa which was uncovered by Lysons gives an unbalanced view of the whole complex, and that unusual-looking structures which have been recorded to the south-east of court B might be farm buildings, perhaps even situated around a third court. Some observers even interpret the buildings in court B as non-domestic, suggesting that the aisled (?) building on the north-east side was a brewery with an adjacent granary. If the villa at Woodchester was associated with agriculture, rather than being a country residence for some high-ranking official, then it must have been the centre for a very large estate in the region.

Although so many villas are known in the county, it is only possible to discuss a handful in any detail, with the result that some quite well-known sites receive only a passing mention. For example, in the parish of Sudeley there are two villas, one at SPOONLEY WOOD and another at WADFIELD. The plan of the SPOONLEY WOOD villa in its final form contains some puzzling elements, and one would very much like to know how this particular villa evolved, but unfortunately it was investigated in the

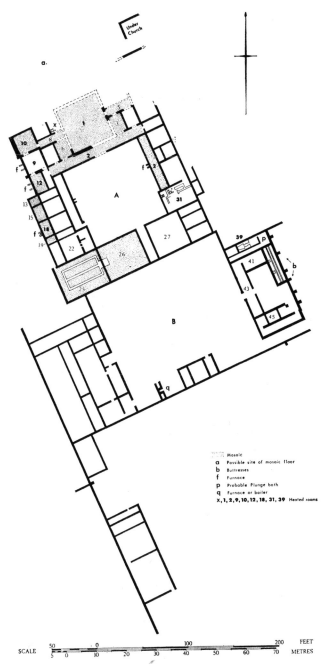

Plan of Woodchester villa/palace.

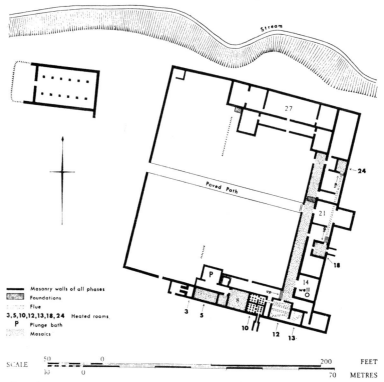

Plan of Spoonley Wood villa.

nineteenth century and such details are not available. The plan shows building on three sides of a courtyard with a bath suite on the south, living quarters on the east and its main reception room in the centre opposite an entrance. On the north side of the courtyard, rooms were laid out as though they were part of a winged corridor villa similar to the plan of Frocester or Farmington. Moreover there was no direct link between the north and east wings, which suggests that they were independent units. Does this imply different social or family units? It can hardly represent a distinction between a farmer and his workers, as the winged corridor range is far too sophisticated for farm workers. It may on the other hand reflect an extended family living within the same complex, the north or subsidiary range being the home of an eldest son and family. An alternative possibility is that the north range constituted the farm office whilst the other rooms were domestic quarters, although this is unlikely because of the quality of the rooms in the north range. Outside the courtyard to the west was an aisled building such as those frequently found in agricultural contexts. In the same parish 2.5km to the west of Spoonley Wood another villa, WADFIELD, was discovered in the nineteenth century of which, again, we know tantalisingly few details. Overall the plan was of three wings around a court with a bath suite in the south range, living accommodation, including the main reception room, on the west and rooms of uncertain use, possibly service rooms, in the north range. A stone building was found in 1968 some 60m to the south. The WHITTINGTON villa in 'Cow Pasture' is better understood, having been excavated more recently. A second-century bath block was replaced during the latter half of the fourth century by a small house with an unusual apsidal room at the south-east corner. Very soon after this house was built, a large detached hall was constructed and linked to the main building by a corridor. Nearly every room in this house was floored with a mosaic, including the large room or hall, which measured 13m by 6m.

The maze of walls found at LILLYHORN in the parish of Bisley with Lypiatt must represent a palimpset of several different periods, and as quite a number of walls remain undetected the whole complex is unfortunately very difficult to understand. From what can be made out the plan looks extremely interesting and unusual. Finds from this site include stamped tiles, a third-century coin hoard of 1223 coins, wall-plaster, but no record of any mosaic. The area covered by walls at Lillyhorn stands comparison with Woodchester.

At CHERINGTON and RODMARTON were Roman buildings of similar size and layout. They were rectangular blocks comprising seven to thirteen rooms and, according to some, had a central courtyard or intra-mural yard; this may show connections with Gaul and indicate a movement of people across the channel at some time in the last quarter of the third century A.D. The presence of heavy flooring and ovens or hearths, however, does not prove it was open to the skies, and it is difficult to see how the remaining rooms could be roofed efficiently if this central area remained open. All the examples of intra-mural yards can be best interpreted as halls.

On the other side of the River Severn in the extreme south of the Forest of Dean at WOOLASTON, Dr. Scott Garrett excavated a villa in the 1930s very close to the bank of the river. In outline the building had the appearance of a winged corridor villa with the addition of possibly two bath suites. Just to the south and detached from the main building was a rectangular structure 10.6m by 4.5m with an elaborately-constructed entrance in the middle of its long west side. A boundary wall 76cms wide emanated from the south-west corner of this building and travelled a distance of 30m before turning west. At the corner a small square structure was found, which, because of the presence of a great deal of charcoal in a ditch in front and because of its shape and size, Scott Garrett interpreted as a small lighthouse. There is the possibility that it was in some way connected with either sea or river craft, although the villa has a distinctly agricultural look and was probably exploiting the fertile soils of the river valley. After turning west, the boundary wall is 65m long on the river side and includes a gate. Against the

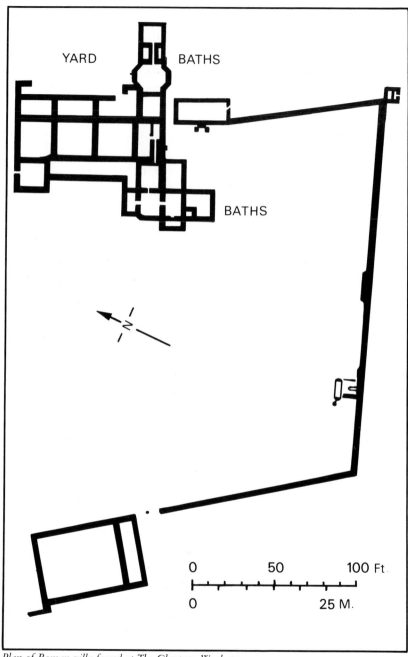

YARD   BATHS

BATHS

N

| 0 | | 50 | | 100 | Ft |

| 0 | | | 25 M. | | |

Plan of Roman villa found at The Chesters, Woolaston.

wall is a small building which may have been a latrine, millhouse or stable. Finally the boundary wall turns north and finishes just short of another free-standing building, possibly an aisled structure. The villa is not thought to have been erected before about A.D. 300, although the presence of second-century coins and pottery may indicate earlier occupation on the site.

It is perhaps appropriate to end this survey of villas with one excavated by the late Mrs. Elsie Clifford, 'the uncrowned queen of Gloucestershire archaeology'. In 1933 she investigated a Roman building at HUCCLECOTE 4km east-south-east of Gloucester and close to Ermin Street, a site which had previously been dug in 1910-11, though no plans or records of that investigation survive to show what was found. However, the 1933 excavation identified the earlier trenches and proceeded to uncover a fairly complete plan of a villa. One of the most interesting facets of the Hucclecote villa often quoted by writers is its early date; Mrs Clifford dates its construction to the second century, which contrasts dramatically with the third- or fourth-century date given to the majority of villas in the region. It was concluded by Mrs Clifford that a first-century timber house was replaced by the stone building around A.D. 150. This however conflicts with the coin evidence included in the excavation report, which states that 'occupation of the site cannot be dated much before A.D. 300'. In fact the pottery illustrated in the report also hints at a later date than put forward by Mrs. Clifford. Whatever the date of its original construction, the floreat of the villa was in the fourth century as the coins, pottery, mosaics and other finds indicate. That there was more than one period of building activity is shown by the number of superimposed floors, some rooms having three. From one of these rooms there comes clear evidence of late alterations being made to the villa. Lying on one tessellated floor, but beneath the latest, was a coin of Theodosius (A.D. 395), which means that life of a reasonably high standard was continuing in the late fourth and probably into the fifth century. Another site in Hucclecote was found in 1957 some 1km south-west of the building just described and was shown to be the badly-robbed remains of a bath block; a stone coffin containing the body of a twenty-five year old female was found close by in the following year.

Most of the agricultural land that was attached to Roman farms has been in continuous use ever since and so the chances of detecting Roman field boundaries are very slender. Ditches seen from the air may be the remnants of field systems, but in the majority of cases it is virtually impossible to date them with any certainty. However, there are a number of places in Gloucestershire where the evidence for Roman fields is most convincing. Field work by P.J. Fowler around the villa at Barnsley Park has revealed over forty hectares of fields, with those immediately adjacent to the villa being enclosed by dry-stone walls. In general the remainder of the field boundaries consist of narrow earthen banks dividing up the land into fairly

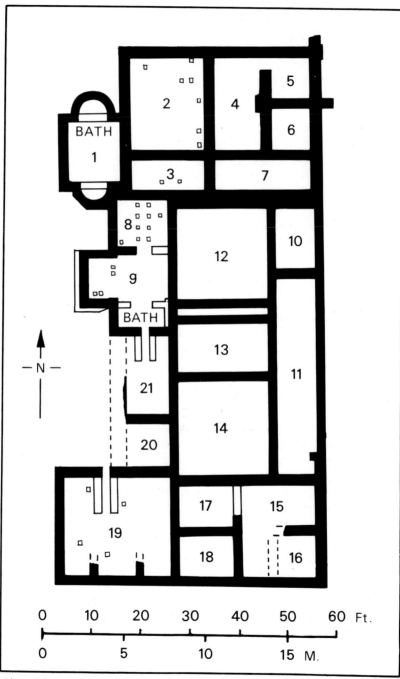

Plan of the Hucclecote villa.

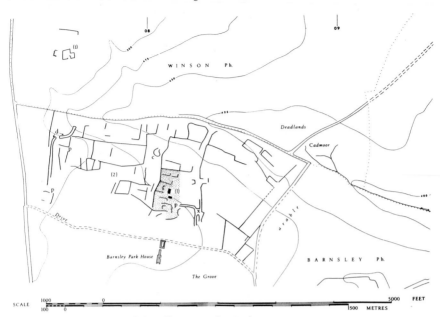

Roman field systems around the villa at Barnsley Park.

regular rectangular plots on the same axes as the villa. The smallest field is about 27m by 52m, which is a ratio of width to length of about 1:2; but the most common unit is about 27m by 82m, that is 1:3. Interestingly the field width of 27m is frequently repeated and may have been a basic unit of measurement when the fields were laid out. It has also been noted in other parts of the country in field systems associated with villas. Pottery from the fields and from two trenches dug across the field boundaries at Barnsley was mainly late-Roman, including grass-tempered ware of fifth- or sixth-century date, none of which surprisingly came from the villa excavations. It therefore looks as though the fields continued in cultivation after the buildings had been abandoned, presumably being farmed from elsewhere. Although there is some doubt as to whether the heavy wheeled plough with a mould-board capable of turning a sod came into Britain during the early Roman period, the size of coulters found at Cirencester and Great Witcombe indicates a fairly solid implement. Arable farming played a large part in the economy of Roman Britain, but it is unlikely that any villa owner made a fortune out of cereals alone. He had a mixed economy and probably made most of his money out of stock-raising with the occasional sidelines, perhaps in timber. Cattle produced meat, milk, cheese, hides and eventually glue! Goats and sheep provided wool which was made into garments that became well known throughout the Roman Empire, and were included in the price-fixing edict of the Emperor Diocletian (A.D. 301). Other animals which

Iron coulter from a Roman plough found associated with building XII, 2, Cirencester, 66 cms long.

have been identified from bones found on archaeological sites include pig, horse, donkey and dog.

The advances made in environmental archaeology in the past decade mean that recently-excavated sites have produced samples for analysis from which it can be ascertained which crops and vegetables were grown. It is not always possible to distinguish between wild and cultivated varieties of plants, but there is evidence for peas, parsnips, turnips, celery, carrots, plums, apples and cherries in Britain. One of the most interesting and earliest examples of this type of study comes from the excavations of a pit in Gloucester in 1893-4, which is said to have produced grape seeds and skins, the remains of wine-pressing. This cannot be verified of course, but it seems more than likely that vines were grown in the region, as they were later in the medieval period.

Very few items of purely agricultural equipment have been found. Most of the farms investigated have produced the usual range of craftsmen's tools one would expect to find, such as knives, chisels, axes and general labouring tools like spades and hoes. Occasionally implements which were used solely in farming have been identified, including the shears from Chedworth, which could have been used for sheep-shearing, and two scythe-like iron blades, about two metres long, which were found at Barnsley Park. These are too long for use by hand and may have come from some form of reaping machine. Once a crop had been cut, it was found necessary on occasions to force-dry it, and several sites have produced structures which are traditionally interpreted as corn driers. They include Eastington, Frocester, Farmington, Kingscote, Lechlade, Lower Slaughter and Upton St Leonards. However, recent experiments at the Butser Farm Project Trust have cast some doubt upon the functions of these driers; in their tests they found that only very thin layers of grain could be efficiently dried, and it seems unlikely that such elaborate driers would have been constructed only to dry small quantities of grain. The alternative interpretation suggests that they were malting floors;

Millstone from Chedworth.

this is supported by the discovery of barley in at least one drier and by the temperature pattern recorded in the experimental version.

Nearly every Roman site, both rural and urban, has produced evidence of the small domestic quern which was turned by hand and used to produce flour for making bread. These were made from a hard stone such as Millstone Grit and Pudding Stone, and sometimes from softer, less efficient stone like the local limestone. Some querns were made from imported stone such as Niedermendig lava from Andernach, and examples of these have also been found in the county. From the villa at Woolaston have come two stones which, because of their size, are described as millstones. They are made of Old Red Sandstone, have a diameter of 76cms and were found reused as material in a floor dated to about A.D. 320. At Frocester a millstone of one metre diameter has also been found and there are others of similar size at Chedworth and Kingscote. Stones of this size could be turned by water power, by animals or presumably by several people.

The picture of farming that emerges in the county and in the south-west as a whole rather differs from that in other parts of lowland Britain, for we find that many villas were not erected until the late third or early fourth century, with the exception of Chedworth and possibly Hucclecote and the bath block at Whittington. Before that date, farms were mainly native in character and continued very much along the lines established before the Roman conquest. Chedworth is earlier than any other villa and may not have been a typical farm. Hucclecote too, if constructed in the second century, may be in a different category, due to its position in the *territorium* of Gloucester. With so few romanised farms in the region before the fourth century, the impact of the Roman cities of Gloucester and Cirencester must have been very dramatic in the rural landscape of the first three centuries A.D. The reason for such a revolution in the countryside around A.D. 300 is not clearly understood, and a number of differing views exist. One body of opinion sees this development of villa-estates centred on a dwelling-house, along with other evidence, as a result of a movement of people from a troubled Gaul in the late third century; another view sees this as evidence of a migration from the towns into the countryside, and only further detailed study and analysis of both towns and rural sites will eventually provide the answer.

5
Work

The majority of working people in Roman Britain were involved in agriculture; on many of the well-organised farms and estates, in addition to the
farm labourers, there were specialist craftsmen who could, for example,
repair and maintain equipment. The majority, during the early years of
Roman occupation, used skills acquired before the conquest and were little
affected by the coming of the Romans, but gradually, with the new demands
created first by the army and later by the local authorities, new crafts and
industries came into existence.

MINING AND QUARRYING

During the first century, when the area was occupied by the army, the
supply of food and materials for equipment was the main preoccupation
amongst the local workforce. A number of the basic raw materials could be
obtained locally and no doubt the iron deposits in the Forest of Dean were
placed under military control initially. For other materials such as lead, tin
and copper one had to look further afield, although the lead works in the
Mendips were quite convenient for troops based at Cirencester or Gloucester.
One lead pig from the Mendips weighing 79kgm and 58cm long has been
found at Syde to the north of Cirencester and is dated to A.D. 79. Like so
many pigs it was stamped on the top, and in this case on one end and side as
well. The main inscription reads IMP VESP AVG VIIII BRIT, telling us that it
was cast when the Emperor Vespasian was consul for the ninth time, that is
in the year A.D. 79. On one end the stamp GPC was impressed five times and
is taken to be an abbreviation for something like GAIVS PVBLIVS C(. . .), an
agent or official acting on behalf of the Emperor and through whose hands
all lead that was produced in the Mendips would have to pass. On one side
was stamped SOC NOVEC, which also appears in different forms on other
lead pigs and can be shown to be short for NOVAEC SOCIETAS, the Novaec
Company. It is known from inscriptions stamped on other lead pigs from
the Mendips that the lead works were under Roman control by A.D. 49, and
that they continued to produce lead throughout the first and second
centuries, the latest stamped pig being dated to A.D. 195-211. Although
there are no pigs of later date, lead continued to be exploited for some time,
mainly for use in the building trade for lining baths and water-pipes and in

Stamped lead pig from the Mendips, found at Syde.

roofing. It was occasionally made into coffins or cremation urns and eventually alloyed with tin to make pewter.

Iron-ore had been exploited from the Forest of Dean since the Iron Age but as each succeeding generation tends to destroy the evidence of earlier workings, it is not surprising that little is known about Iron Age and Roman activity in the Forest. The road pattern in the area suggests that access to the Forest was of some importance. Iron-working has been positively identified at Lydney and suggested at the Scowles between Lydney and Bream. Workings perhaps related to the extraction of iron-ore have been located to the east of Cinderford, 18kms west-south-west of Gloucester, where a great deal of iron slag, pottery and a possible furnace-base have been found at Chestnuts Hill and Popes Hill. Material from Boughspring included what was described as 'bloomery slag', but its date is uncertain. At Lydney Park there is clear evidence of Roman iron-mining which is still visible to this day. The earliest occupation on this promontary dates to the first century B.C., and there are finds which suggest that there was some form of activity during the first and second centuries A.D. However, it was during the third century that there was a marked increase in activity on the site, as reflected by the coins found during the excavations directed by Sir Mortimer Wheeler in 1928-9. During the last quarter of the third century a series of primitive wooden huts was being lived in, beneath one of which Wheeler came across the shaft of an iron-mine. For 5.5m the shaft was open, about 1m wide and 1.5m deep and then it became enclosed forming a tunnel. The fill of the shaft consisted of large pieces of rock, presumably the miners' debris. Short pick-hammers appear to have been used as the incisions left by them were found in the mine, but no actual examples were discovered during the excavations. However, a model pick, 8.7cms long across the head and possibly a toy, was recovered from the floor of a late third-century hut. Further work was done at Lydney in 1959 by Dr. C. Scott-Garrett when a mine adit was found, on the roof of which were more pick marks. The use to which iron was put was very varied. Nearly all the tools used in agriculture and by building craftsmen were made from iron. Other metals were exploited by the Romans such as tin and copper, but there are no deposits in this area and supplies were brought from elsewhere such as Cornwall or Wales.

In pre-Roman times any stone that was required could have been found outcropping in the Cotswolds, and similarly, when the army wanted stone for making roads, much of it could have been found without a great deal of quarrying. However, by the end of the first century, when the cities of Gloucester and Cirencester were founded, vast quantities of stone were required, and the opening of quarries to supply this need must have had a dramatic effect on the landscape. The regular stream of wagons to and from the quarries would also have been an unusual sight to those who could remember the countryside before the Roman occupation. The demand for stone continued in the urban centres throughout the second century for public buildings, houses, shops, streets and defences. When Cirencester was ringed with a wall, Mr. Wacher calculates that for the 4km circuit some 84,000 cu metres of stone were needed. As with all extractive industries it is difficult to find remains of the earliest workings in an area which has been exploited over a long period of time. It has long been suspected that the bumps and hollows around the amphitheatre at Cirencester, in an area known as the Querns, were the remains of Roman quarrying, but it is only in the past few years that positive evidence has come to light to show that this was so. Excavations in the former kitchen garden of The Querns by Mr. T.C. Darvill showed, for the first time in Gloucestershire, details of the techniques used by the Romans for extracting good-quality building stone. The original working face of this Roman quarry had been stepped so as to recover blocks of stone. These were removed by using wedges or picks, the marks of which were found on the remaining faces of the quarry. They were 1cm in diameter, and where they occurred in groups were 3-5cm apart. Another Roman quarry almost certainly existed south-east of the amphitheatre, where a near vertical quarry-like face, now covered with trees and bushes, still stands some 30m high to this day. Many other quarries must have existed, supplying stone for Gloucester, Kingscote and the other larger settlements, and eventually, of course, for the construction of villas. A possible quarry was located at Brimpsfield. In addition to stone, supplies of lime, sand and gravel were necessary as well as timber for scaffolding, flooring, posts, doors and the framework of roofs.

The trading of local stone with other areas of Britain was not great. It may

Marble statue from the Spoonley Wood villa.

have been used for the tombstone of Julius Classicianus, the procurator sent to Britain after the troubles of A.D. 60/1 who died in office and was buried in London. Stone from elsewhere was used for specialised purposes. Some roofs were covered with sandstone 'slates' from either the Forest of Dean or the Bristol region, instead of the more usual limestone, either because Cotswold slates were no longer being produced or were more expensive. Stone used for making mosaic floors was generally local and included oolitic and lias limestone and sandstone, although on occasions Purbeck marble and Kimmeridge shale were employed. Purbeck marble was also used in making the tombstone of Julia Casta found in Cirencester, and Bath stone for that of Rufus Sita at Gloucester. Imported stone has been found on several Roman sites, the most common probably being marble from the Mediterranean, which has been found at Ebrington, Cirencester and Gloucester. The marble sculptures found at Woodchester and Spoonley Wood were almost certainly imported already carved. Niedermendig lava from Andernach was used for querns and examples have been found at Kingscote, Whittington and Cirencester. Coal has been found in Roman contexts on a number of sites, including Dryhill, Compton Abdale, Frocester, Great Witcombe, Lower Slaughter and Whittington. It could have come from Somerset or the Forest of Dean.

BRICK- AND POTTERY-MAKING

The large-scale digging of clay also made its mark on the Roman landscape. It was required for pottery, bricks, roof-tiles, red *tesserae* and a number of less common items such as pipes, roof-finials or those peculiar nine-sided objects that have been found at Kingscote, Frocester and Uley. The ready availability of good-quality stone capable of being cut into building blocks meant that fired clay was seldom used in the building trade except for roofs. No brick was used in the city walls at Cirencester or Gloucester and it has rarely been found in houses or shops, except in hypocausts. However, despite its limited use, Roman brick is found on the majority of sites in the county and recent studies have enabled us to understand more about the organisation of brick-making and the distribution of the products. The local brick-makers' custom of stamping some of their bricks with groups of letters has proved of particular value. At Gloucester there was a city brickworks operating from the beginning of the second century, producing tiles and bricks which were stamped with the letters RPG, and, on occasions, the names of the magistrates who were responsible for the brickworks. It is thought that the letters stand for REI PUBLICAE GLEVENSIUM. The bulk of the RPG stamped bricks have been found in Gloucester, although others have been noted outside the city proper, probably from the territory that was attached to the *colonia*, at Dryhill, Frocester, Hucclecote, Ifold, Upton St. Leonards and Great Witcombe. During the excavations of St. Oswald's

Stamped tiles from Gloucester.

Stamped tiles from the Cotswolds.

Priory in Gloucester, many tiles and bricks were found, along with other evidence to suggest that the kilns which produced them were not far away.

As well as official brickworks, there were private operators who followed the pattern of stamping their products. The stamps seem to be abbreviated forms of names. Some are obviously names, such as ARVERI which refers to *Arverus*, who was making tile and brick mainly for Cirencester, and it is suggested that the rest are a short-hand way of writing a romanised name, which generally consisted of three parts (*tria nomina*). One group contains the letters TPF with additional letters such as TPFA, TPFB or TPFC, perhaps signifying different workshops within the brickworks. Other groups of letters include TCM, VLA (or VCA), LHS, LLH and LLQ. The reason for the brick-makers of Gloucestershire stamping their products when it was not done to any extent in the country at large is not apparent, but it is possible that they followed the lead given by the municipal works in Gloucester, which was copying a tradition long established in other parts of the Roman Empire.

No brick kilns have been found in the county, although there is good reason to believe that kilns existed in the vicinity of St Oswald's Priory, Gloucester and possibly at Deerhurst. The nearest known ones are at Leigh Sinton (Hereford and Worcester) and Minety (Wiltshire). Here, 10km south

A reconstruction of a typical Roman tile kiln.

of Cirencester, was the main brickworks of the area and one of the biggest
civilian works yet found in Roman Britain. Only two of the possible ten or
so kilns have been uncovered, and they conform to the general plan that one
expects for such a kiln. A large part of the structure was built below ground
and consisted of a square or rectangular combustion chamber, above which
the over floor was supported on a series of closely-spaced walls in the
chamber, which themselves were carried across the main central flue by
arches. No details of the superstructure have survived, but it was almost
certainly temporary in nature. The brick-makers at Minety might, on
occasions, set up temporary works nearer to the demand, if suitable raw
materials and fuel could be found in the area.

Roman roof-tiling consisted of the flat *tegula* with raised sides, over
which was placed a curved *imbrex* to prevent rain from seeping between.
The *imbrex* may also have served as a ridge-tile, and there may have been a
terra-cotta finial on the ridge made in the same kiln as the tiles. Bath suites
and rooms with underfloor heating required ordinary tiles in the construction of *pilae* for supporting the raised floors and for lining flues, and
specially-made box-flue-tiles which were built into the walls. Tiles were
being supplied to Cirencester by the end of the first century and at
Kingscote stamped tiles of the TPF series were being used during the first half
of the second century. By the fourth century, builders were tending to use

natural stone slates for roofs, and channelled hypocausts were replacing those which required a large number of tiles, all of which suggests that the production of tile and brick was at a very much-reduced scale, if not totally abandoned.

Some brick-makers engaged in pottery-making, and there is evidence to suggest that this happened at Minety, but so far large-scale pottery-production centres have not been found in the county. One particular type of pottery known as Severn Valley ware, (later to be made in other places outside the county), originated in the region. It was made by small groups of potters working from a diversity of centres, beginning some time around 60s A.D., as indicated by its discovery at Kingsholm and in levels pre-dating the construction of the fortress at Gloucester. By the end of the second century the ware was reaching Hadrian's Wall and during the third and fourth centuries the industry continued to flourish, eventually coming to a halt at some time towards the end of the fourth century. One possible site where Severn Valley ware was produced, although probably on a small scale, was found during survey work in advance of the M5. At Alkington a small updraught kiln was found associated with Severn Valley ware and dated to the early/mid-second century A.D. A distorted tankard, possibly a waster, of this ware has been found in Cirencester and may reflect the presence of a kiln not far away from the town. Eventually more kilns are likely to be found, perhaps not far from the main centres of population. Although it is not clear whether the production of Severn Valley ware was stimulated by the needs of the Roman army, this was the reason for the growth of Savernake ware, which is to be found mainly in Wiltshire and southern Gloucestershire. Savernake ware is quite common on first-century sites in Cirencester, but was later replaced by black-burnished ware from Dorset, which became common on all sites and maintained its dominance over other coarse wares during the third and fourth centuries. There must also have been some local small-scale producers of everyday wares, some of which are gradually beginning to be recognised.

The more expensive best-quality tablewares were imported in the first two centuries A.D. From France during the first century came the well-known red-gloss samian pottery along with some glazed pots from such areas as the Allier Valley and colour-coated wares from Lyons. In the second century samian continued to be imported, and a bronze colour-coated ware from the Rhineland now began to feature on the pottery stalls in Gloucestershire markets. However, not all fine ware was from abroad for by this time the Nene Valley products were beginning to reach the area. By the early third century the fall in imports of samian ware coincided with an increasing use of British fine wares, and by the mid-third century pottery from the Oxfordshire kilns became very significant in the region and continued to be so during the fourth century, becoming, in Cirencester, one of the two major sources of supply. In the second half of the fourth century a calcite-gritted ware became widely available in the area and probably continued to be used well into the fifth century, when other wares were no longer produced. A hand-made pottery containing chopped vegetation incorporated with the clay and generally known as grass-tempered ware may have been used in the fifth and sixth centuries, but some argue a later date for the making of this particular type. It has been found in small quantities at Cirencester, Barnsley Park, Uley and Kingscote, but much more reached Frocester. A great deal more has yet to be learnt about pottery-making in the fifth century, if, indeed, it continued to be produced at this time.

Besides the Alkington kiln, the only other pottery kilns which have been investigated were found when the College of Art in Brunswick Road, Gloucester, was being built in 1966-7. They were situated outside the defences of the fortress and *colonia* in an area which, judging from the amount of coal and iron slag associated with intensive burning, was frequented by craftsmen and set aside for some of the town's unsocial industrial activities. Parts of two kilns were recorded and shown to be of a similar design. They were circular, about one metre in diameter and each had a pedestal projecting from the back of the combustion chamber to support fire-bars, which in turn carried the oven floor. Only one fire-bar was found and nothing remained of the oven floor. Once the kiln was loaded with unfired pottery, it was covered with a temporary roof made of clay, some of which was recovered from the excavations and seen to carry the impression of straw. Another interesting feature was the discovery in the kilns and from all over the site of fired clay tubes or pipes. None were complete, but the largest section was 20cms long and ranged in diameter from 7.5 to 12.5cms. They may have acted as insulation tubes around the perimeter of the oven, or they may have conducted air more rapidly from the combustion chamber to the outside of the kiln. A wide range of pottery including dishes, bowls, beakers, jars and flagons came from the site, and one *mortarium* was stamped with the name of *A Terentius Ripanus* who may have been working at Gloucester between A.D. 60-90. The date of the kilns given by the excavator is between A.D. 70-110, with a preference being shown for the first two decades of that period.

Pottery was often transported by water but, in the absence of suitable rivers, the only means of moving it from the potteries to the markets was by cart or wagon along the road system. It is, therefore, not surprising to discover that the everyday cheap pottery used in Cirencester came into the town from the south along Ermin Street, rather than from potteries to the north and north-east, in which case carts would have to negotiate the Cotswold escarpment before reaching the south of the county. For the more expensive or specialised type of pottery, traders were quite prepared to tackle long and difficult journeys, with no doubt corresponding adjustments

Reconstruction of a mosaic craftsman's workshop in the Corinium Museum.

to the price. *Mortaria*, or mixing bowls, reached the county from a variety of sources depending upon the date; for example, the potteries centred around Mancetter and Hartshill in the midlands began to send *mortaria* in quantity in the second century.

MOSAICS

Two raw materials already discussed were combined in the construction of mosaic floors: fired clay was used for red *tesserae* and naturally-occurring stone for other colours. The mortar required for laying such a floor meant that the mosaicist also needed supplies of lime and sand. Sometimes other materials were used to bring out special features. Red glass was used in the Seasons pavement from Cirencester to depict blood from Actaeon's wounded leg and in the flowers around the head of Spring. The hare pavement found in Beeches Road, Cirencester, used green glass to bring out slight variations in colour on the hare's back. There were, broadly speaking, two ways of laying mosaic floors. First, they could be laid directly in a room on to a prepared mortar bed upon which guide lines had been painted or scored in the damp mortar. A skilled craftsman needed very few of these to enable him to complete a simple floor, although one can see problems with something the size of the Woodchester pavement. Red lines reflecting the blue all-over meander pattern of the mosaic were found under the floor of the changing room in building XII, I, Cirencester, and in several places in the town heaps of debris, resulting from making *tesserae* on site, have been found. Secondly, a mosaic might be constructed in prefabricated sections in a workshop and then transported to the site, to be pieced together in the room. Evidence for this method is hard to come by, but some of the errors found in mosaics may have resulted from such a technique.

The earliest mosaics in Britain are those found at Fishbourne and dated to *c.* A.D. 75-80, with designs which indicate that the craftsmen were immigrants from Italy or Gaul. By the middle of the second century mosaics were being laid in town houses and villas by local craftsmen who introduced different designs from their continental counterparts. Gloucestershire has long been famous for its Roman mosaic floors, and fortunate in having antiquarians who recorded and published drawings of floors discovered over the past two hundred years. Samuel Lysons (1763-1819) recorded floors from Cirencester, Colesbourne, Great Witcombe, Withington and Woodchester and published coloured drawings at the beginning of the nineteenth century. Buckman and Newmarch, with commendable speed, brought out a book with coloured engravings in 1850, only one year after the discovery of two mosaics in Dyer Street, Cirencester. Not all early records include illustrations, and some references to mosaic floors may be to plain tessellated pavements. Even so, the number listed is impressive and stands comparison with any other part of Roman Britain, particularly in Cirencester, where around eighty mosaics have been noted. In Gloucester, which in area is much smaller than Cirencester, the number is less, there being just over twenty known. We find mosaic floors first being laid in town buildings in the middle of the second century, which is the date given to the fragmentary remains of a mosaic found in 13-17 Berkeley Street, Gloucester (building I, 18). Several in Cirencester date from about the same time, including the Seasons and Hunting Dogs pavements from building XVII, 1 in Dyer Street. But clearly the high point of the mosaicist's craft was in the fourth century, when elaborate floors were being laid in both villas and towns.

The similarity in design and the repetitive nature of certain motifs make it possible to identify the products of one particular firm, which, because it is

The Orpheus pavement from Woodchester.

assumed that their workshops were based in *Corinium*, is referred to as the Corinian school. Not all fourth-century mosaics show the hallmarks of the Corinian school and some may have been designed and laid by firms from elsewhere. However, one of the Corinian school's best-known designs is that depicting Orpheus, and pavements of this sort have been found at Withington, Woodchester, Barton Farm and Dyer Street, Cirencester. Undoubtedly that at Woodchester is the most well known and arguably the finest mosaic in Britain. It is the largest in north-west Europe, measuring 15m square with the central circles contained within a square of 7.5m. The central feature is lost, but around that were two concentric bands, an inner one of birds and an outer one of prowling animals. The band of birds is interrupted by a figure playing a lyre interpreted as Orpheus. The pavement from Barton Farm is of very similar workmanship and design, but here the

Gryphon on the Woodchester pavement.

Leopard on the Woodchester pavement.

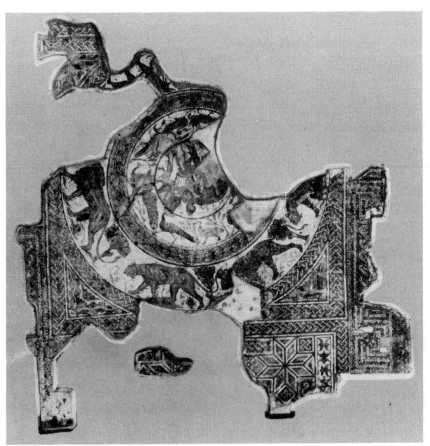

The Orpheus pavement from the Barton Farm villa, Cirencester.

central medallion depicting Orpheus is almost complete. The mosaic from
Dyer Street, Cirencester, is known only from a drawing and, although of a
similar design to those already described, contains some unusual features
such as the mysterious figure above Orpheus in the centre.

   Another group of mosaics laid by craftsmen from the local workshop can
be found in two fourth-century buildings in *insula* XII, Cirencester. Building
XII, 1 had at least five mosaics, two of which were very simple, consisting of
a panel of red *tesserae* set in a white background. The small mosaic from the
changing room of the bath suite was very similar in design to the panel at the
east end of the main east-west corridor at Woodchester. The all-over
meander in blue *tesserae* can be traced from a single band of *tesserae* into two
bands and finally three. It then follows a meander pattern before finishing

TESSELATED PAVEMENT DISCOVERED AT Nº 93, DYER STREET, CIRENCESTER. A.D. 1820.

The Orpheus pavement said to have been found in Dyer Street, Cirencester.

beside the point where the single band started. In the main living rooms of this house were two fine floors, the best known of which is the hare mosaic. Connecting the hare mosaic with an already-existing floor in the main body of the building was an exquisite panel containing a central cantharus or two-handled cup, either side of which is a long-tailed bird, possibly a peacock. The hare mosaic, which is later than the other two in this building, almost certainly dates from the closing years of the fourth century. In building XII, 2 there were at least nine mosaics, only seven of which remained *in situ* to be found during excavations. Again there were similarities with other mosaics in the region, indicating that these floors were probably from the Corinian school. An earlier example of a town house, with mosaics dating mainly to the second century, was found in Dyer Street, Cirencester, where mosaics

The Seasons pavement from Dyer Street Cirencester as now displayed in the Corinium Museum.

discovered over a long period, beginning in 1783, have given us some idea of the manner in which the wealthy person decorated his home at a time when stone houses were first appearing. This house, XVII, 1, probably had the best collection of 'carpets' of any so far excavated in Britain. They include the Seasons and Hunting Dogs pavements, the fourth-century Orpheus floor and one which shows great workmanship, the so-called marine scene.

There are quite a number of tantalising references to what must have been impressive mosaics from Gloucester, but very few details or illustrations have survived, and recent excavations have not produced as many well-preserved floors as at Cirencester. A floor found in 1914 in Northgate Street, now on display in Gloucester City museum, features in the centre a cantharus, around which are panels of guilloche mat and stylised flowers. Excavations prior to the construction of the market hall, conducted by John Rhodes and Mark Hassall in 1966-7, recovered parts of three mosaics, of which the most complete seems to show a central panel of Bacchus riding on a leopard and is dated to the fourth century.

Besides the great Orpheus pavement at Woodchester, many other rooms and corridors there had mosaic floors, one of which carried two short inscriptions and is therefore of extra interest. This square mosaic consisted

E

The Seasons pavement, Cirencester. Detail of the Goddess of Corn, Ceres.

The Hunting Dogs pavement from Dyer Street, now in the Corinium Museum.

Samuel Lysons' drawing of a mosaic floor found in Dyer Street in 1783 and known as the marine scene.

of five octagons, one in each corner and one in the centre. The most complete corner panel shows two naked boys holding a basket of fruit above their heads and beneath them the inscription *Bonum Eventum* — 'Happiness to you'. In the opposite corner only the beginning of an inscription survived, but it has been restored to read *Bene C(olite)* — 'Enjoy yourselves'. The only other known mosaic in the county with an inscription was found in the Lydney Roman Temple. Above a scene depicting fishes and dolphins is a slightly-damaged inscription which has been restored to read:- *D(eo) N(odenti) T(itus) Flavius Senilis pr(aepositus) rel(iquationi) ex stipibus possuit o(pus cur)ante Victorino inter(pret)e.* 'To the god Nodens, Titus Flavius Senilis officer in charge of the supply-depot of the fleet, laid this pavement out of the money offerings; the work being in charge of Victorinus, interpreter on the Governor's staff'. The mosaic is dated to the late fourth century.

The best group of mosaic floors still to be seen *in situ* is at Chedworth. That in the dining-room comprises a large octagon containing panels with Satyrs and Maenads, and in the outer corners is a representation of the four seasons. There are mosaics associated with both bath suites, but the best preserved are in the west range. There are of course many other mosaics in villas in the county including Great Witcombe, Wadfield, Withington,

Mosaic floor found on the site of the New Market Hall in 1966 showing Bacchus riding on a leopard.

Mosaic with an inscription from the temple at Lydney Park.

Mosaic floor from the main reception room of the Chedworth villa.

Frocester, Colesbourne and Ebrington. The only mosaic to have come from one of the larger settlements is from Kingscote; this has now been lifted and is on display in the Corinium Museum.

WALL-PAINTINGS

Walls were most likely decorated by a different group of craftsmen, for none of the significant patterns which occur on mosaic floors appear on wall-paintings. However, the dado occasionally echoes the border of a mosaic as it seems to in the piece from the Compton Abdale villa, or in the black and white Greek fret at Chedworth. Gradually our knowledge of such decoration is improving and already it is possible to see regional variations and, perhaps, schools of wall-painters. Quite large sections have been recovered from excavations at Cirencester and more recently from Kingscote. One section from Cirencester came from building XXIII, 1 where a large expanse was found to be still standing to a height of 1.8m on an early second-century wall. This was rescued from the site and is now displayed in the Corinium Museum. The design consisted of panels of yellow divided by dark-green columns on which were painted white patterns. Beneath these panels was a dark-blue dado upon which a repetitive pattern in red and white had been

Panel from a mosaic floor found at Withington showing Neptune flanked by Dolphins. The panel is not rectangular.

painted. The Kingscote wall-plaster contained figures as did the plaster from the villa at Colesbourne, sometimes known as Comb End. We are again indebted to Samuel Lysons for recording this wall-plaster when he visited the site in 1779. All that survived was the lower part of the wall showing the feet of several individuals interspersed with pillars. The figures are depicted in black outline, shaded in red, on a white background.

FURNITURE

Very few examples of the furniture once used in town houses or villas have been found. Kimmeridge Shale was often used for small tables and some pieces have occurred in Britain, but none are known from Gloucestershire. Perhaps small side tables made from stone were preferred; several slabs of stone with chip-carving decoration have been found and interpreted as table tops. A bow-fronted example has come from Cirencester and rectangular ones from Gloucester, Whittington and Chedworth (2). Bone hinges used in cupboards, chests and small boxes have turned up on many sites and, along with various metal fittings, are the sole evidence for these items of furniture, which must have been commonplace in houses of any substance.

SCULPTURE

The range of subject matter and style in Romano-British sculpture from Gloucestershire is far greater than for any other part of the country. At one end of the scale are the imported marble sculptures, such as those found at Woodchester and Spoonley Wood, and at the other the clearly native pieces

Altar found at Kings Stanley.

carved from the local stone which can be found on many of the sites in the county. Many of the local pieces are votive in character and help us to understand the religious life of the people living in town and country. Stone-carving was a craft which was not restricted to the carving of busts and religious items; the sculptors were also employed to carve elaborate architectural pieces. There are far too many pieces of sculpture and decorated architectural fragments for all to be dealt with in these pages and reference will only be made to a few, but the reader is strongly urged to visit the collections housed in Gloucester and Cirencester museums in order to acquire a feel for the quality of carving, which can only be appreciated by seeing the objects at first hand. One piece deserves a special mention as it is one of the few examples from Roman Britain which name the artist. It was found during quarrying at Custom Scrubs, Bisley and is a votive tablet, some half a metre high, depicting Romulus, in the guise of Mars, standing in a niche on which has been carved the inscription

DEO ROM(U)LO GULIOEPIUS DONAVIT IUVENTINUS FECIT

which means

'To the god Romulus Gulioepius presented this, Juventinus made it'.

Tombstone to Philus found at Cirencester in 1836.

Another votive tablet came from the same place depicting a tunic-clad figure, and, although not signed by anybody, it has all the appearances of having been made by the same craftsman, Juventinus. We also know the name of another stone-carver who dedicated an altar found in Cirencester. He was called Sulinus, the son of Brucetus, and is known to have been a sculptor for he is described as such on an inscription from a statue-base found in Bath.

Amongst some of the earliest pieces of sculpture to appear after the Roman conquest are the outstandng examples of military tombstones from Wotton and Cirencester and one of Philus, a civilian, from Cirencester. The military gravestones were probably not carved by local craftsmen, but by provincial military personnel who came to Britain with the army. The tombstone of Philus is 2m high and shows a portrait of the deceased wearing a *cucullus*, a hooded cloak reaching to his knees, standng between two columns topped with Corinthian capitals. Again this piece looks as though it was carved by an established artist rather than by a local craftsman beginning to feel his way with romanised sculpture. A recurring theme on sculpture from the county is that of Mars as god of agriculture. Five altars have been found at Kings Stanley, four of which portray Mars, either in his classical pose or as a more native-looking unhelmeted figure. Other native forms of Mars have been found at Lower Slaughter and Cirencester. Five altars from Bisley show the figure of Mars, in one case mounted on a horse, and he is portrayed on an altar from Hazlewood and two votive tablets from Custom scrubs. Carvings showing Mother goddesses of the *Genii Cucullati* were also a popular subject for the sculptors working in the county.

OTHER OCCUPATIONS

In addition to the craftsmen already discussed, there were others who provided a service to people living in towns and to the surrounding farmers. For example, at Cirencester, a fragment of a crucible containing gold specks was found on the site of the market hall in insula II, indicating a goldsmith working in the town, probably making jewellery. From the north-west corner of insula VI in Cirencester, amongst a mass of animal bones, was clear evidence of bone-working in the form of rough-outs for pins or needles. People were also employed in bronze-working, furniture-making and a host of other crafts. Oculists were working at Cirencester and Lydney where stamps they used have been found. The majority of shops are likely to have been run by their owners, but additional help may have been required. The baker, for example, probably employed several people to assist with the mundane tasks in the preparation of bread, and others no doubt did the same. Quite a number of people were required to service such places as the public baths and amphitheatre; to work for the local council in maintaining roads, drains, water supply and waste-disposal and to do general routine work on buildings and property owned by the council.

6
Communications

One of the prime considerations for an army of occupation is to secure its lines of communication, in order to ensure that supplies of food and equipment can be maintained and men deployed to new centres of activity without delay. As soon as the legions had begun to fan out across Britain after the triumphal march into Colchester headed by Claudius, they began both to construct roads as they advanced, and to seek suitable places for the Roman navy to anchor and unload its cargo. Roads are notoriously difficult to date by the usual archaeological methods because coins, pottery and other artefacts are rarely found in the road make-up or in the side ditches. Consequently most roads are dated by their relation to sites with an established chronology. For example, it is thought that Ermin Street is slightly earlier than the Fosse Way because of the way these two roads relate to Cirencester; Ermin Street represents the initial advance of the Roman army into the county and links the fort at Cirencester with that at Kingsholm, whereas the Fosse Way was probably constructed soon after. It is quite remarkable in that it stretches in an almost straight line from Lincoln in the north-east to Exeter in the south-west, a distance of some 400kms. This road can be traced through the county fairly easily, as modern roads tend to follow the same line. Here and there the two deviate, as on the hill into Stow-on-the-Wold, where a short stretch of the original road has been uncovered for many years, but at the time of writing is badly overgrown and the sign is barely visible. South-west of Cirencester the Fosse Way survives as a green lane where it follows the county boundary for 11km. Likewise portions of Ermin Street and Akeman Street can be traced through the county and occasionally the *agger*, or bank upon which the road was built, can be seen. Akeman Street appears clearly in fields in the parishes of Quenington and Coln St Aldwyns, and in 1952 a trench was dug across the road to reveal an *agger* of rammed gravel 9.5m wide with a central channel and kerb-stones. It seems likely, therefore, that Ermin Street, the Fosse Way and Akeman Street were first constructed by the army to provide communication between different units and their forts and fortresses. As the military command remained in the area for some thirty years, the roads became a permanent feature and were maintained when the army moved on. It is also possible that the road between Gloucester and Sea Mills (now in

The Fosse Way near Easton Grey looking towards Cirencester.

Avon) was constructed during these early years, linking the fortress at Gloucester with the military installation at Sea Mills. Ryknild Street branches from the Fosse Way just to the north of Bourton-on-the-Water and heads for the Roman settlement at Alcester in Warwickshire.

A Roman road from *Ariconium* (Weston-under-Penyard, Herefordshire) can be traced through the Forest of Dean to Lydney, and at Blackpool Bridge 2.4km north-west of Blakeney, a length of metalled road, 2.4m wide and edged with sandstone kerbs, is exposed. To the north-east of the village of Lydney it joins the main coastal road between Gloucester and Caerwent, which itself eventually goes to the West Gate of Gloucester and, somewhere along the way, is joined by a road from the settlement of Dymock. The course of the road from the North Gate of Gloucester is uncertain for the first part, but eventually it can be traced leading to the Roman settlement at Worcester.

The size and composition of Roman roads varies considerably from one part of the country to another, and even the make-up of a single road can alter a great deal over a relatively short distance. With the aid of equipment such as the *groma*, which could be used for laying out straight lines and right angles, surveyors marked out a line across the countryside in straight sections, with slight changes of direction being made when necessary on high spots, which were used as sighting points by the surveyors. Difficult natural obstacles were treated individually, and the road was designed to suit the local situation, by curving around a hill side, by digging terraces or cuttings, or by making the road zig-zag down steep slopes. Such a treatment was necessary when Ermin Street descended the escarpment at Birdlip, between Cirencester and Gloucester. For the roads built with military considerations in mind, land was requisitioned; in peaceful times, however, the local council had to make arrangements with landowners before roads were constructed. Such roads probably evolved through constant use rather than being deliberately created, and only when the volume of traffic was sufficiently high and of the sort which required good roads, were the local authorities obliged to step in and regularise matters. Much has been said and written about the possibility of land around the *coloniae* of Britain (the *territorium*) being divided into regular plots for the retired legionary soldiers living in the city. Such a system, generally known as centuriation, would have had a grid of roads and tracks, such as is known from some cities elsewhere in the Roman Empire. Work is underway examining the possibility of centuriation around Gloucester, but it is too early to state with certainty whether or not it existed. There are some who believe that such a system was never instigated in Britain.

The study of roads in Britain and throughout the Empire is greatly helped by a document entitled *Itinerarium Provinciarum Antonini Augusti*, usually referred to as the Antonine Itinerary, which is a list of some 225 routes along the roads of the Empire, fifteen of which concern roads in Britain. This document is known to us today as a post-Roman copy and, as such, contains a number of copying errors made by scribes at different times which have been brilliantly detected by Professor Rivet. Each route in the Itinerary is headed by the names of the places at the beginning and end together with the distance between each. The only route which is of interest to roads and settlements in Gloucestershire is Itinerary XIII. This is headed *Item ab Isca Calleva, m.p. CVIIII* which is the route from *Isca*, Caerleon, to *Calleva*, Silchester, a total mileage of 109 Roman miles. (In a Roman mile there were 1,000 *Passus* of five *Pedes* each, and, using the generally accepted figure of 11.65ins or 296mm for the value of a *Pes*, this gives a figure of 1618 yards or 1480 metres for a Roman mile). The Itinerary is as follows:-

ITER XIII   *Item ab Isca Calleva, m.p. CVIIII*

Itinerary name	Roman miles	Location
Burrio	9	Usk
Blestio	11	Monmouth
Ariconio	11	Weston-under-Penyard
Clevo	15	Gloucester
Durocornovio	14	Wanborough
Spinis	15	Woodspeen
Calleva	15	Silchester

There is an obvious discrepancy between the stated mileage of 109 in the heading and the sum of the distances given in the list above, which is ninety miles. Cirencester is not mentioned and it looks as though in transcribing the Itinerary the city of Cirencester has been omitted. By inserting a stage of nineteen miles after Gloucester the figures then tally. But what is the purpose of the Antonine Itinerary? It was thought for a long time to have been a list of official routes for the imperial post *(Cursus Publicus)*, but doubt has been cast on this interpretation and Professor Rivet's study of the British section of the Itinerary supports the view that it was a 'collection of journeys which were made or planned at different dates by different people.'

As well as the main arterial roads with metalled surfaces and side ditches which have left their mark on the landscape, there were scores of other minor roads or tracks which linked the smaller settlements with each other, or the villas with the main roads. Some of these may have been metalled; the word *straet*, used in Saxon charters, indicates a properly-laid road surface rather than a dirt track. These and other local roads which have been discovered by intensive field work are shown on the plan. In addition, there is an increasing number of ditched tracks observed from the air as crop marks mainly on the gravels of the upper Thames in the south of the county. If this pattern is repeated throughout the county then the number of roads and tracks which originally existed must have been considerable. After all, every farm and settlement had a track connecting it with the main road system or some local road, and, if we postulate more settlements than traditionally believed, there must have been a corresponding number of roads and tracks enabling farmers to travel to and from market.

The most detailed and systematic excavation of a Roman road in the county was undertaken at Cirencester between 1971-2, when an area 40m by 12m was opened up to investigate the road which leads from the Cirencester Bath Gate and is considered to be the Fosse Way. The latest road surface exposed consisted of a much-worn metalled layer of small limestone. There were many ruts on it, some of which had been patched by in-filling with

The Fosse Way just outside Cirencester showing ruts caused by heavy use.

The kerbed edge of the Fosse Way.

limestone of different character from that of the road itself. Clear evidence of how much a road surface suffered at the hands of weather was demonstrated when the excavations were left open during the winter, and the surface quickly broke up. By comparison with the town streets, where, when a street became badly worn, a new surface was laid on top, there were surprisingly few layers of different surfaces in this particular stretch of road. Here they must have used the road until it was virtually worn out, judging by the accumulation of road silt on either side, in places up to a metre deep. When this silt was removed, the edge or kerb of the road became visible, revealing distinct changes of direction in alignment. The road was probably built in the late second century and continued in use into the fifth century, serving a cemetery as well as the amphitheatre. Other sections of road have been investigated at Bourton-on-the-Water and at Kingscote.

There were probably more bridges taking roads across rivers than traditionally believed, but few have been found. Clear evidence of a bridge was uncovered just outside the Verulamium Gate at Cirencester, and there may have been one at Bourton-on-the-Water where the Fosse Way crosses the Windrush. There must have been others, including several in the vicinity of Gloucester, carrying roads across the River Severn.

No Roman milestones have been found in the county except for a possible one, now lost, said to be Roman and found at Eastington, but there are some 110 from Britain as a whole. They usually have an inscription which records the emperor's titles, the place from which the road measurements were made, and a mileage figure. No doubt these handy lumps of stone standing beside roads were acquired for building or as gate posts fairly soon after the Roman period, when of course the details carved on the stone would be unintelligible.

Along these roads and tracks travelled a variety of wheeled vehicles, packhorses, pedestrians and groups of animals. A fairly common object found on archaeological sites is the lynch-pin, used to keep the wheel in place on the axle of the carts which carried produce to market and returned with supplies for the farm and its household. Cattle and sheep were driven to market on foot, as they were until quite recent times, and on market days at certain times of the year the roads leading to the main markets such as Cirencester bustled with activity. Smaller markets may well have existed in some of the other settlements like Lower Slaughter or Kingscote. As well as the purely local traffic, roads carried vehicles which were bringing goods from further afield and taking specialised goods to a wider market in the country and even, in some cases, for export; good-quality pottery was being traded over a wide area and in the county we find material from the Nene Valley, Oxfordshire and the New Forest and imported fine wares.

Shallow draft barges were probably used to transport commercial goods by river, as they are today in different parts of the world. The Severn with its tributaries, including the Avon, was clearly navigable for some way, and in the south of the county the Thames could have been used up to Lechlade and possibly as far as Cricklade, at which point goods could have been transferred to carts for distribution along Ermin Street. As indicated earlier a thriving port was situated at Gloucester, where part of a wooden quay has been found. Here goods for export were loaded on to sea-going vessels, and likewise, imports were received direct from the countries of their origin.

7
People

Personal details of people who were living in Britain during the first five centuries A.D. come from two main sources: from their physical remains it is possible to determine their height and general appearance, and to gain some idea of defects and injuries incurred when alive; other information has to be gathered from written accounts, very few of which have survived from Britain, as in most cases they were on organic material which has totally decomposed in the ground. More formal information, however, was often carved on stone and has survived. Such inscriptions include those on official buildings, tombstones, milestones and altars. Occasionally people engaged in the practice, often considered to be a twentieth-century phenomenon, of scribbling on walls or doodling on wet pottery and brick before it was fired. These *graffiti* can be very informative, and give insights into everyday life which the more formal inscriptions do not.

We have already seen that two sculptors have left their names on pieces of work: Juventinus, who carved the two votive tablets found near Bisley, and Sulinus, who is recorded on two inscriptions. An altar from Cirencester says *To the Suleviae, Sulinus, son of Brucetus, willingly and deservedly fulfilled his vow*, which on its own does not tell us very much about Sulinus, other than that his father was Brucetus and that he dedicated an altar to the Suleviae. However, the fact that his father's name is known from this altar makes it certain that it is the same Sulinus who is recorded on a statue-base found in Bath, which says *To the Suleviae, Sulinus, a sculptor, son of Brucetus, gladly and deservedly made this offering*. The name suggests that Sulinus was born in Bath and named after Sulis.

The earliest inscriptions are on the military tombstones discussed in our first chapter. Although these commemorate soldiers who were born outside Britain, there is an inscription from Rome which records a legionary soldier of the sixth legion, born in Gloucester and from a family which was granted citizenship from Trajan between A.D. 98-117. Another recruit to the Roman army was an auxiliary who came from Gloucester. Part of his discharge diploma was found at Colchester, and although his name is not complete it was probably Saturninus. He was discharged from the *coh. I fida Vardullorum* in A.D. 154 or 159. Another local person is recorded on a

Altar from Cirencester erected to Sulinus.

similar diploma, this time from the Roman province of Pannonia, modern
west Hungary. This refers to Lucco, son of Trenus, a Dobunnian, who was
discharged from the *cohors I Britannica milliaria civium Romanorum* in
A.D. 105 and who was presumably recruited before the army left this area in
the late 70s. Professor A.R. Birley has recently drawn attention to an altar
found in Cirencester bearing the name Sabidius Maximus, and suggests that
he is the same person as the one commemorated on an inscription from
Macedonia which records his military service of 40 years in, among others,
the *Second Legion Augusta*. Why he should have dedicated an altar in
Cirencester, and the reason for his presence there in the second century,
remains a mystery.

The earliest civilian tombstone is that dedicated to Philus, set up in the
first century A.D. in the same cemetery as the auxiliary soldiers were buried
in, to the south of the fort at Cirencester. He came from Gaul and was
probably a trader following in the wake of the Roman army. He was aged
forty-five when he died in Cirencester. A group of four civilian tombstones
was found together in Cirencester in 1971, three of which carried full
inscriptions telling us about some of the people living in the city. The
youngest person mentioned was Aurelius Igennus who was six years and ten
months old when he died. The tombstone was erected by his father Aurelius
Euticianus who may have been of Greek origin. A certain Comitinus had a
gravestone erected to Lucius Petronius who died aged forty, whilst
Nemmonius Verecundus, who is recorded on the third stone, lived to see his
seventy-fifth year. He was not, however, the oldest person from Gloucestershire to be recorded on a tombstone, for an official from Gloucester had a
monumental tomb built in his memory at Bath, on which it was recorded
that he died aged eighty. Perhaps he was on a visit to the spa for medicinal
purposes, or, which is more likely, had retired there. Woman are also
recorded on tombstones: at Cirencester, Julia Casta was buried aged thirty-
three; Publia Vicana's memorial was put up by her husband Publius Vitalis;
Casta Castrensis is commemorated on another stone, and Ingenuina was
responsible for erecting a tombstone to her husband. This latter tombstone
is in Gloucester Museum, but it is now known that it came from Cirencester.
A tombstone found near Horsley was to Julia Ingenuilla who lived for
twenty years, five months and twenty-nine days! One of the highest-
ranking Roman officials known to have been based in the region is mentioned on a rectangular base for a column found in 1891 in Cirencester. This
states that a statue and column were restored by a person whose first two
names were Lucius Septimius and who was described as governor of
Britannia Prima, one of the fourth-century provinces of Britain. His
presence in Cirencester is usually taken to imply that the city was the capital
of that province.

Messages intended only for the gods give an interesting insight into

Inscription from Bath recording Sulinus a sculptor.

people's lives in the fourth century. From the Roman temple at Uley have come over 200 *defixiones*, that is small sheets of lead upon which a curse has been written. After the message had been written, the piece of lead was rolled up and firmly squeezed together before being nailed in place in the temple. Unrolling these curses is extremely difficult, because after prolonged burial the lead becomes brittle, but currently the work is being undertaken by the British Museum. The first three to be dealt with from the excavations have been studied by M.W.C. Hassall, and two of his translations are given below. The curses are sometimes written on both sides and usually in a cursive script. One measuring 13.5cms by 8.5cms relates to a stolen animal and reads:-

> *Cenacus complains to the god Mercury about Vitalinus and Natalinus his son concerning the draught animal that was stolen. He begs the god Mercury that they may neither have health before they repay me promptly the animal they have stolen and (repay) the god the devotion which he himself has demanded from them.*

A woman by the name of Saturnina lost some linen, or, as she claimed, had it stolen, and pleads for its return with the promise of a reward to the gods.

> *A memorandum to the god Mercury from Saturnina a woman concerning the linen cloth she has lost. Let him who stole it not have rest until he brings the aforesaid things to the aforesaid temple, whether he is man or woman, slave or free. She gives a third part to the aforesaid god on condition that he exact those things which have been aforewritten. A third part from what has been lost is given to the god Silvanus on condition that he exact this, whether (the thief) is man or woman, slave or free . . .*

Although doctors dealing with general ailments must have worked in the larger urban centres, we have no evidence of this other than some possible medical instruments. On the other hand, we know the names of three eye specialists, because the stamps which they used to mark their prescriptions have survived. Two of these stamps have come from Cirencester and one from Lydney, where it is to be expected that a variety of medical people were based to deal with the problems of the visiting sick. Instructions for the user, together with the oculist's name, were cut in reverse on stone, up to four different stampes often being cut on to the sides of an oblong block about 3 cms long. The prescription, upon which the stamps were impressed, was solid and available in small sticks. From Cirencester came the following stamp with four different instructions:-

An altar from Cirencester bearing the name Sabidius Maximus.

Civilian tombstones found at Watermoor, Cirencester.

> *Atticus' frankincense salve*
> *For all pains to be made up with egg*
>
> *Atticus' mild (salve) for all pains*
> *After the onset of inflammation*
>
> *Atticus' (salve) of poppy*
> *To be made up for all pains*
>
> *Atticus' alum salve to be*
> *made up for granulation*

Another one from Cirencester has only two messages:-

> *Minervalis' alum (salve)*
> *for all pains*
>
> *Minervalis' incense (salve)*
> *for the onset of inflammation to be*
> *made up with egg*

The stamp from Lydney records a prescription of Julius Jucundus and three different ways of using it: in drops, as an ointment mixed with honey, or as a tincture to be applied with a brush.

An oculists stamp from Cirencester, 4.5 cms long.

As well as the more formal stamps on bricks and tiles, *graffiti* were occasionally inscribed while the clay was still wet. One from Cirencester tells us that 'Candidus made . . . roofing tiles' and another from Barnsley Park simply has the word TVB(V)L meaning 'box-tile(s)'. Attempts at the alphabet seem fairly common, and occasionally single words appear with very little obvious meaning, presumably written by some of the people in the brickworks who had an elementary knowledge of Latin. A piece of plaster from the villa at Hucclecote has an outline drawing of a building inscribed on it, hardly a builder's plan, but probably a doodle, or possibly even a sketch of a house. It shows a pitched roof and what appears to be some form of arcading at a lower level. There are no details of windows or doors. The name Firmini was found carved on a building stone at Barnsley Park, possibly the name of the stone mason scratched on in an idle moment. Alternatively, it has been suggested that this was the name of one of the owners. The information that we can extract from this sort of evidence is very meagre. We have names, birthplaces, some idea of positions held by a few people, and a range of ages at death, but the sum total is small indeed compared with the number of people who lived in the county during the Roman period.

Physical details can be deduced from a study of skeletal remains, and gradually we are beginning to build up a picture of people's physical appearance and condition during the first four centuries A.D. It is for this reason that more attention has been paid recently to the excavation of cemeteries with the hope that, from a reasonably large sample, one can draw conclusions and apply them to the population at large. The organisation of cemeteries and details of burial rites are explored in a later chapter; for the present we are interested in the people who were buried there. At present the only large group of skeletons is from Cirencester, where over 450 were found during excavations prior to the construction of the western relief road around the town. These have been extensively studied by the late Dr. C.

A piece of plaster from Hucclecote showing a sketch of a house.

Wells. Even as many as 450 skeletons constitute quite a small sample of all those laid to rest in the graveyards around the town and upon which to draw general conclusions. Assuming an average life span of forty years, in 400 years the population would have been replaced ten times. The population of the town was not static, but is likely to have been in the region of 5-10,000 which, over 400 years, would produce between 50-100,000 dead. However, for the first hundred years or so, the rite of cremation was the main, if not the sole means of disposing of the dead, reducing the number of skeletons that could be found. However, even a conservative estimate would give at least 50,000 inhumations somewhere around the town, although many have doubtless been destroyed since. These figures mean that the sample of 450 represents less than one per cent of the town's population over the period of the Roman occupation.

One of the most striking facts to emerge about the cemetery outside the Bath Gate at Cirencester from which these skeletons came, is that there were two and a half times more females than males. There is no evidence from studying the distribution of male and female burials to suggest that there were separate areas for each, and the imbalance between the two remains a mystery. Not all of the skeletons were sufficiently complete to be used in calculations of height or age at death, but of the one hundred and seven male skeletons an average height of 5′ 6½″ (1691mm) was deduced and for the forty-four females it was 5′ 2″ (1579mm). It is difficult to obtain meaningful

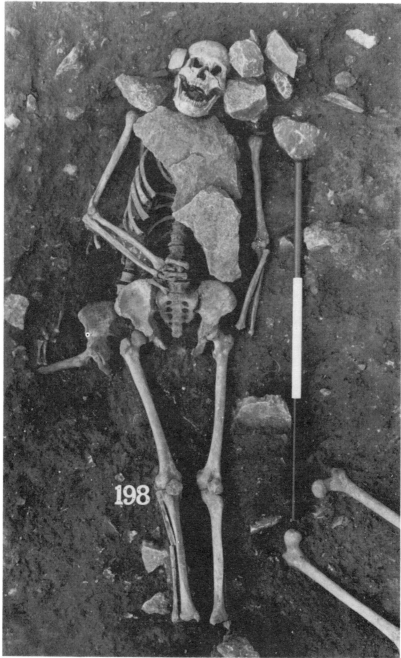

A skeleton from the cemetery at Cirencester.

present-day averages, but the above figures appear to be only slightly smaller than contemporary European man. The tallest male noted was 5′ 11″ (1817mm) and female, 5′ 6¾″ (1698mm). In comparison, the analysis of skeletons from a cemetery outside York showed the average height for men to be 5′ 7″ (1702mm) and for women 5′ 1″ (1549mm), which is fairly close to the figures obtained from the Cirencester cemetery.

Diseases are not particularly easy to diagnose in skeletal remains, but the commonest of those identified was arthritis, which was found in eighty per cent of the bodies. This condition is the result of a succession of injuries, often of a very minor kind, which are repeated over many months or even years. In effect it reflects wear and tear on the joints and can provide useful information about life styles and even occupations. It occurred in the spine of men, woman and juveniles, which is a sure indication that they were commonly carrying out heavy tasks, but the joint most widely affected by arthritis was the hip, followed by the shoulder. The overall picture which emerges is of a people leading physically strenuous lives in which they were often exposed to a great deal of strain over long periods. The most notable congenital defect found was spina bifida, which was detected in five skeletons. Fifteen per cent of the skeletons exhibited fractures, but strangely there were eight times more breaks in females than in males. Rib fractures were common, and there were breaks in legs, arms, fingers and foot bones, but none were detected in the jaw or neck. By contrast there were only two skeletons which showed conclusive evidence of a dislocation, which in both cases was to the shoulder. Dr. Wells was able to show during his examination that at least six people, one of whom was a woman, had been decapitated from behind, using a weapon which must have been razor sharp. A collection of wounds inflicted by either a blunt instrument or a sharp weapon were found.

Details of infections are not easy to detect from a study of surviving bones, although there was some evidence to suggest that poliomyelitis was present amongst these people. There were also three cases of gout, one of which was severe. It is possible to make estimates, albeit not particularly reliable ones, of how many children a woman had; with the thirteen skeletons from which it was possible to make the necessary measurements, a mean of 4.7 children per woman was deduced. Allowing for infant mortality this suggests an average of two to three children per family.

The state of the teeth of the inhabitants of Cirencester was extremely good, judging from those found in the cemetery. Women lost fifty-six per cent more teeth than men in spite of the fact that, on average, women died three years younger, suggesting a lower standard of oral hygiene among the female population. As the number of bad teeth is closely related to diet, the fact that there was a relatively-low decay rate at Cirencester implies that good supplies of meat were available, and that not too much reliance was

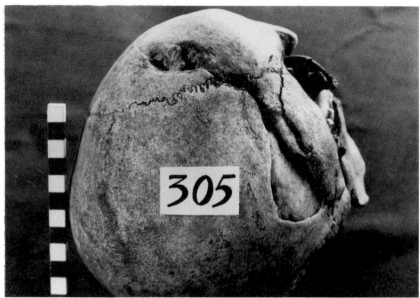

A skull from the Roman cemetery at Cirencester.

placed on carbohydrates. There was no evidence of dental filling, ornamentation or use of false teeth, and the only dentistry practised appears to have been limited to occasional extraction of decayed and painful teeth.

A particularly interesting skeleton had quite severe cranial wounds, and Dr. Calvin Wells, who studied the skull, wrote the following:-

> This man had received a severe gash into his right parietal which, as well as incising the bone, had fractured it so that a triangular area had become separated from the rest of the parietal and was depressed inwards towards the meninges. Despite the severity of the injury it eventually healed firmly, but is likely to have caused various neurological after-effects. There is also an elliptical opening with smoothly bevelled sides, in the superior part of his frontal bone. This appears to be a trephination. It was probably performed therapeutically in an attempt to relieve symptoms which had been caused by pressure on the brain from the depressed triangle of parietal.

A number of experimental projects were carried out on a sample of the skeletal material from Cirencester, one of which produced some quite remarkable results. This involved determining the quantity of lead present in the bone of the skeletons, for it has been shown that a high bone-lead concentration indicates heavy exposure to it during a person's lifetime. The results of this work have shown that, of the sample tested, the majority had been heavily exposed to lead when alive and some on a massive scale. Lead was used for water pipes in Britain, but no examples have yet been found in Cirencester, and, even if such pipes were used, the temporarily hard waters of the Cotswolds would have deposited a protective coating inside the pipes after a relatively short time. Lead vessels were not used for cooking, and in the absence of lead pollution in the atmosphere, the most likely source was the diet.

8
Religion

The toleration of a wide range of religious practices in the Roman world, and the considerable freedom of individuals to worship gods of their choice lead to the existence of many different religious cults in Britain, ranging from the newly-introduced classical to long-established native ones. Worship took place both in the privacy of the home as an integral part of family life and at the numerous public temples and shrines. Temples have been found at Chedworth, Lydney, Uley and Wycomb, but, surprisingly, none have been positively identified at Gloucester or Cirencester, where quite a number must have stood. The sites of other temples or shrines in the county are hinted at by collections of sculpture and votive objects, such as those found at Lower Slaughter, Daglingworth, King's Stanley or Bisley. Buildings, sculpture, altars and inscriptions all contribute to our understanding of the religious practices which once existed in the county.

TEMPLES AND SHRINES

Quarrying 1km east of the villa at Chedworth has uncovered Roman pottery and building stone on a number of occasions, but it was not until 1926 that excavations were carried out on the site. Then W. St. Clair Baddeley found that, despite the fact that much stone had been carted from the site in 1864-5, several courses of Roman walling survived, outlining an almost square building measuring 12m by 12.1m internally. Several of the stones noted by Baddeley were enormous for such a small building, being 1.2m by 0.6m in size and part of a wall 1.5m thick. A small projection at the south-west corner was probably part of an entrance, a buttress, or, perhaps more likely, part of a small annexe. It seems from what Baddeley found that this was a temple of a type frequently seen in Celtic regions. Coins from the site, which indicate activity in the second century, may date its construction. Parts of a column, a Tuscan capital, a stone entablature and other pieces of dressed stone indicate the quality of the architecture. With columns which are thought to have been at least 3.6m high and unusually wide walls, the temple probably rose above the surrounding trees to be seen over a wide area. The association of many votive objects with a building at Wycomb (no. 15 on plan) has lead to the suggestion that it was a temple, although there are some who do not accept this interpretation on the evidence as it stands. The

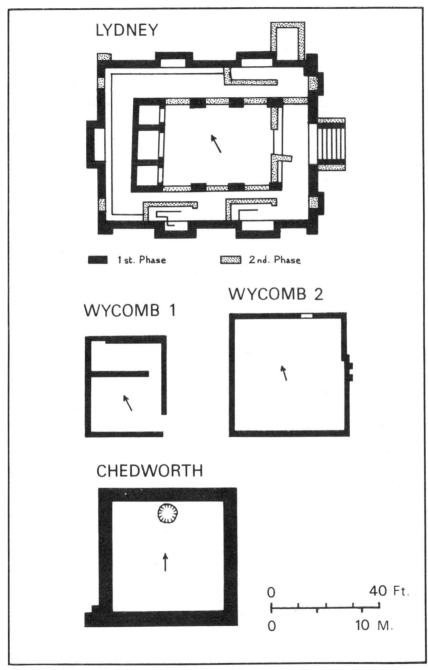

Plans of temples found in Gloucestershire.

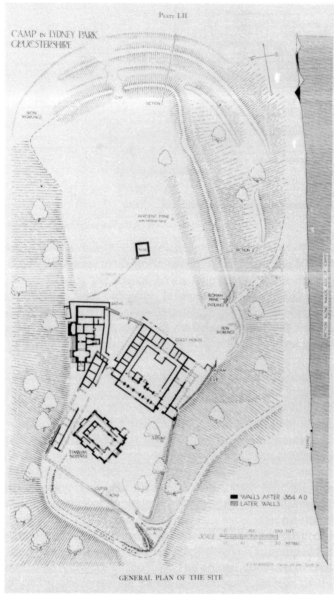

Plan of buildings in Lydney Park.

structure was 13.5m square and had a raised stone floor in the centre. An earlier building 'underneath may also have had religious connotations (no. 16 on plan). This was rectangular, 9m by 11m and was divided into two by a wall one third of the way along the main axis, in which there was a door linking the two sections, placed not centrally but against the east wall. From the area came votive objects and many coins, and there is sufficient circumstantial evidence to suggest that these two buildings may have served as temples. Furthermore some have interpreted other buildings found nearby as shrines, suggesting that the whole site at Wycomb may have had a more religious function than previously thought. The votive objects from the site include two stone panels, each originally with three figures (one of which depicted the *Genii Cucullati*, several other unidentified stone figures, a bronze statuette of Mars and a model bronze axe.

In the late fourth century a temple and other buildings were constructed within the fortifications of the earlier hill-fort at Lydney Park and apparently dedicated to the god Nodens, a god of hunting, a water god and, more significantly, a god who had healing powers. The whole complex was contained within a wall with the temple in the southern half of the enclosure. North-east of the temple was a large courtyard house and to the west of that a bath suite. Between the temple and the baths was a long narrow building containing a dozen or more rooms leading off a corridor. The date given by Wheeler for this complex was arrived at by the discovery of coins, sealed beneath the buildings, which pointed to some time after A.D. 364, although the possibility that this date records extensive building modifications and that the original foundation was earlier should not be overlooked. Excavations to help determine this point were carried out by Dr. J. Casey in 1980. The temple was basically rectangular measuring 18m by 24m overall with projecting bays in the outer wall. The main entrance was on the south-east side and there were two smaller doors at the other end. In all there were seven bays contained within the outer wall along which there ran a stone bench. The central part of the temple, the *cella*, was originally formed by six piers with three shrines at the north-west end, but after a collapse, various modifications to the temple took place, including the construction of enclosing walls in front of three of the projecting bays or chapels, and the filling in by a wall between the piers of the *cella*. Some mosaics were laid at this time, including one in the *cella* which carried the inscription already referred to.

North-east of the temple was a large building 40.5m by 48.7m and reminiscent in plan of some of the larger town houses. It consisted of three wings around a central courtyard with, rather unusually, a large hall on the fourth side. The dating evidence from this part of the site is consistent with that from elsewhere and assigns a date after A.D. 364 for the initial construction with modifications taking place after A.D. 367. The north-east

F

Artist's reconstruction of the temple complex at Lydney Park.

and north-west wings comprised a series of living rooms with a slightly larger one in the centre of the north-east wing opposite an entrance porch from the courtyard. On the south-east side of the courtyard was a long room, the entrance of which was characterised by a monumental gateway and may have been for carts and waggons to deliver goods for use within the building. The front of the structure consisted of a long hall 26m long and 4.7m wide internally with heavily-buttressed piers along the length of the hall, which may have been designed to carry an upper storey. The most likely function of this building was to provide accommodation for visitors to the shrine, a fact supported by the provision of a large bath building to the north-west of the guest house. Being just over 40m long, this was only a little smaller than the baths at Wroxeter and of a similar size to those at Caerwent. The existence of such a building clearly not intended for private use adds further weight to the idea that the courtyard house was for travellers to the temple rather than the residence of some individual. The entrance to the baths was by means of a corridor which connected with the so-called 'long building'. The main rooms conform to the usual pattern for such a building, being arranged so that the temperature gradually increased as one moved from one room to another. Attached to some rooms were baths which could contain either hot or cold water depending upon their position. A small group of heated rooms, to the east of the main ones but attached to them, may have had a similar arrangement whereby steam percolated through, or they may have been for dry heat. There was a latrine in the building and 35m to the north-east a stone-built tank 5.8m square, the floor of which was made of sandstone slabs covered with cement. From its southern corner ran a stone-lined conduit from which were found iron collars used to join together the wooden water-pipes which supplied the baths. The outside walls of the baths were rendered in cement or plaster finished in a deep crimson surface, as were many of the internal walls, although the colour varied in the different rooms. Floors were paved with stone slabs and covered with plain cement or *opus signinum* or, in at least one case, a mosaic. The 'long building' formed the north-west side of the lower half of the walled enclosure, running close by the temple and, at the north-eastern end, joining with the baths. It was 56m long and consisted of a range of rooms, a number of which had mosaic floors, opening on to a verandah or corridor. It is generally thought that these were living rooms rather than shops and were for the use of those requiring to be cured by the healing-god.

The sum of the evidence indicates that after A.D. 364, or slightly later, the building of the settlement as a single unit was begun. The courtyard, house, baths and long building appear to have been linked with the temple and designed to provide residential accommodation for visitors to the site in search of a cure. There were many small objects found both during the excavations of 1928-9 and from the earlier nineteenth-century excavations and casual diggings. These include 300 bronze bracelets, 320 pins, forty or more bronze spoons and many more, all presumably offerings made by visitors to the gods. On top of this over 6,000 coins have been found from this fairly small site, indicating the commercial aspect of temple life. That it was the god Nodens who was the cult figure in this temple complex is indicated by various items from Lydney, including a piece of lead, a mosaic, and two bronze plates which all carry inscriptions to him. There are a number of other objects associated with the cult, including ten representations of dogs in stone and bronze. The outline of a dog also appears on one of the bronze plates dedicated to the god. Forty-five bronze letters, each pierced with a nail hole and measuring between 5cms and 8cms, were probably connected with votive inscriptions put up by visitors to the temple.

It is possible that one of the villas discussed earlier was not a farm, but, like Lydney, had a religious significance. This is the view that Dr. G. Webster has of Chedworth, where he believes that the building contains too many rooms and that the baths are too elaborate to have been concerned

A bronze plate with nail-hole and punched inscription which reads 'To the god Mars Nodons, Flavius Blandinus, drill-instructor, pays a vow'. From Lydney.

solely with agriculture. He cites the small shrine or *Nymphaeum* at the north-west corner of the complex as further evidence to support his ideas. The water supply which fed the site was originally contained within a reservoir at this point, but in the fourth century an octagonal basin was built and contained within an apsidal building. An uninscribed altar and a column came from within the building, which is interpreted as being a shrine to a water-goddess. It continued to have special significance after the conversion of the owners to Christianity, for a *chi-rho* symbol was carved on one of the stone slabs which formed the rim of the octagonal reservoir. Until Dr. Webster presents his arguments in detail it is perhaps unwise to embark upon any detailed discussion of the merits of this suggestion; suffice it to say that the complex does not compare in scale with Lydney, nor is the religious building at Chedworth the focus of the settlement or contemporaneous with the other three ranges of buildings.

The most recently-and extensively-excavated religious complex is that at West Hill, Uley, which was investigated between 1977-9 by the Committee for Rescue Archaeology in Avon, Gloucestershire and Somerset, under the Direction of Dr. Ann Ellison. Here the earliest structures were prehistoric, with a significant phase of timber building in the late Iron Age, probably

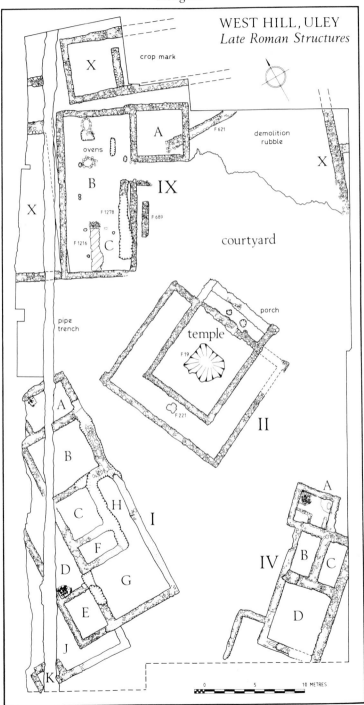

WEST HILL, ULEY
Late Roman Structures

crop mark

X

F 621

demolition
rubble

X

ovens

A

B

IX

X

F 1278

F 689

F 1216

C

courtyard

pipe
trench

temple

porch

F 19

F 221

II

A

B

C

H

I

A

D

G

IV

B

C

E

D

J

K

0   5   10 METRES

Plan of late Roman buildings excavated at Uley.

dating to the first half of the first century A.D. The absence of domestic material and the votive nature of some finds indicate that it was almost certainly used for religious purposes. In the second century two stone buildings (IV and X on plan) were erected and are thought to have been connected with a temple, as yet unlocated. Then in the second quarter of the fourth century a stone-built temple was constructed. In plan this was almost square, measuring 14m by 12m, with a central *cella* and an ambulatory on three sides. The entrance was on the fourth, north-east side where there was a wooden porch. A worn cobbled floor was found in the ambulatory, but none was found in the *cella* where there was a large hole 3.5m across containing some 500 coins, in which the excavator thinks there may have been a sacred tree or post, or even a water container, implying that the *cella* was open to the skies. Against this theory are the facts that such an open area in the temple would collect rain water and become unusable, and also that, as there is no obvious sign that the area was drained, it must have been roofed. The debate will continue and may never be resolved in this particular case. Two masonry buildings (I and IX) were built at about the same time as the temple, one of which (I) may have provided accommodation for priests or visitors, or even have served as the temple's shop where worshippers could purchase votive offerings. The other had some living accommodation as well as areas which may have been used for the storage and preparation of food. Rubbish from the temple was spread out over the demolished remains of buildings I, IV and IX which meant that many objects associated with the temple's use have been preserved, including over 200 lead curses (*defixiones*), two of which have already been described. Also recovered were items of sculpture in bronze and stone and two altars depicting Mercury flanked by a goat and cockerel, which, taken together with the text of the curses, indicate that the main cult was the worship of Mercury. This is supported by the analysis of one quarter of a million animal bones, showing that goat and sheep were common and that domestic fowl was also present in significant proportions; the associates of Mercury were the goat, ram and cockerel. At some time around A.D. 380 part of the entrance and north-east corner of the temple collapsed, and a masonry structure was erected over the remains of the corner (VIII). Meanwhile the rest of the temple remained intact and continued to be used in some form or other into the fifth century. Post-Roman structures were also found, and there are slight hints that some of these may have had Christian connections.

The only other site where structural remains of a possible religious complex are known is at Sapperton, 5.6km west of Cirencester, where aerial photography has provided the outline of what might have been a temple enclosure and an associated building. Three banks and two ditches enclose an approximately 55m square area from which field walking has produced evidence of walls, tile and pottery. There is an entrance on the east side,

Aerial photograph of Sapperton.

beyond which is a building which could be interpreted as a priest's house.

At Bourton-on-the-Water several circular buildings have been found which may have had religious connections, although none have produced any votive objects to support this interpretation. However, at Lower Slaughter the remarkable collection found in a well, along with the discovery of columns, must indicate a religious building in the vicinity. Outside the major settlements, the discovery of groups of religious sculpture indicates the sites of shrines or temples. From Daglingworth have come two votive tablets and a dedication slab; from King's Stanley five sculptured altars; from Bisley a further five altars and from Custom Scrubs two gabled votive tablets portraying Mars. A timber octagonal building at Upton St. Leonards may have been a shrine.

One of the most interesting indigenous cults in the area is that of the *Genii*

Stone relief of GENII CUCULLATI found at Cirencester.

Stone relief of the THREE MOTHERS from Cirencester.

Cucullati, godlets of fertility, healing and the other world. They are shown on sculpture wearing a hooded cloak *(cucullus)* either singly or, more usually, as a group of three. Carvings of the *Genii Cucullati* have been found at Cirencester, Lower Slaughter, Daglingworth, Wycomb and Whittington. Sometimes the group of three is depicted in company with a Mother Goddess. This deity, who featured prominently in Celtic religion, is also often represented on sculpture as a group of three figures and is found all over Britain and particularly in Gloucestershire. There are four pieces from Cirencester depicting the Mother Goddess, and one with a seated Mother Goddess and *Genii Cucullati*. Only one of the four shows a single goddess, in this case seated in a chair holding fruit. A votive tablet depicting three Mother Goddesses was found in the Wotton-under-Edge or Kingscote region, and another, not far away over the county boundary at Easton Grey, Wilts, appears to represent three male worshippers approaching a Mother Goddess and is signed by the artist, *Civilis fecit.*

CHRISTIANITY

Although it was not until A.D. 312 that the Emperor Constantine made Christianity the official religion of the Empire, the cult had spread into the Roman provinces much earlier, as shown by Alban's stand at Verulamium at the beginning of the third century A.D., for which he became the first British martyr. Representatives from the British church are known to have attended a meeting in Arles in the year A.D. 314 and one of them may have come from Cirencester. If so, then Christianity must have played a sufficiently important role in the town to have its own church. Archaeological evidence to chronicle the spread of Christianity in the county is sparse and by no means definite. The most widely-quoted piece is the famous word-square or cryptogram scratched on wall plaster and found in Victoria Road, Cirencester in 1868 which reads:-

```
R   O   T   A   S
O   P   E   R   A
T   E   N   E   T
A   R   E   P   O
S   A   T   O   R
```

and if translated produces a rather meaningless phrase, 'the sower Arepo holds the wheel carefully'. Other examples have been found in the Roman world and are now generally considered to be of Christian significance, the religious element being carefully hidden so as not to arouse suspicion at a time of persecution. The letters of the square can be rearranged to form a cross, leaving two sets of the letters A and O which can be seen as alpha and omega, 'the beginning and the end'.

```
                P
  A             A             O
                T
                E
                R
      P A T E R N O S T E R
                O
                S
                T
  A             E             O
                R
```

Three examples of the *chi-rho* monogram, another Christian symbol, have been found on stones at Chedworth, some being in their original position. These symbols, along with the word-square, constitute the sum of our evidence reflecting Christianity from the county. The fourth-century mosaics showing Orpheus, a theme adopted by the early church, are thought by some people to be connected with the spread of Christianity.

There is also a suggestion of a link between the siting of parish churches and earlier Roman villas; Roman buildings are known beneath churches at Frocester, Kings Stanley and Woodchester, and not too far away at Bitton, Brookthorpe, Chedworth, Dodington, Poulton and Swell. Such a link may be purely coincidental, or simply due to the availability of already-cut building stone. At present there is no proof of continuity of Christianity on any of these sites from the Roman period, but it is a point which will repay further study.

BURIAL CUSTOMS

People of Roman Britain were concerned with ideas of an after-life, a feature of both Celtic and Classical religions, and the burial of the dead in a proper manner was of prime importance to believers. The recent excavations of a large cemetery at Cirencester and the reappraisal of burial grounds around Gloucester mean that we are better able to discuss burial practices. It is still basically correct to say that cremation was the main method of disposal of the dead practised from the time of the conquest until the mid-second century, although evidence from the Gloucester district of third- and fourth-century cremations, along with examples from elsewhere in Britain, shows that the practice had not been entirely abandoned by the end of the second century. Apart from in the cemeteries around the major settlements, cremations have been found at Ampney Crucis, Dodington, Lechlade, Minchinhampton, Notgrove, Temple Guiting and Whittington. The body was placed on a funeral pyre, and after burning the ashes and any unburnt bone were collected and placed in a container, generally a pot, which was then frequently sealed with some form of lid. These pots were then usually placed in a pit dug in the ground, covered with earth and their position indicated by a marker above ground. Sometimes they were placed in a hole especially cut into a block of stone, frequently a disused piece of building stone. One such piece was found in London Road near St. Catherine's Church, Gloucester, where a hole had been carved in the base of an inverted column, into which had been placed a second-century pot containing a cremation. The marker above ground ranged from something fairly simple in wood to elaborately-carved tombstones, such as those already described at Wotton that were set up in the first century to the memory of soldiers. This cemetery contained both cremations and inhumations and seems to have served both military and civilian populations. Some of the cremation pots belonged to the third century showing that the practice died hard in this part of the country. Graves for inhumations contained nails, indicating the use of wooden coffins; the discovery of hobnails shows that the dead were often buried with their shoes, a feature noted in the Cirencester cemetery. From the site of St. Margaret's Hospital, Wotton, walls were found which might have been part of a late funerary building.

An extensive cemetery lay to the east of Gloucester, where over thirty-seven skeletons were found in 1966 when the College of Art was being built in Brunswick Road, and in 1974 a small limestone coffin with a lead lining and containing the remains of an infant was found outside the Co-operative store. At Kingsholm a late Roman cemetery containing cremations existed, one burial of which contained fifth-century military equipment. There were other cemeteries outside the *colonia* along the roads leading from the main gates, as Roman law forbade the burial of bodies or cremated ashes within the town. This was also the case at Cirencester, where cemeteries have been found outside all the major gates to the town; the biggest of these lay beyond the Bath Gate in an area once used for stone-quarrying. Excavations there between 1969-1978 have produced 453 burials, including three cremations and one unique burial which consisted of a shallow grave-pit containing nails, ash and the burnt bone of an adult male, giving the impression that the coffin had been placed in a grave and burnt *in situ*. The alignment of the graves in this cemetery was determined by existing tracks and boundaries, as was the case in most Roman cemeteries until Christian burial rites required an east-west orientation. Of the 450 skeletons, 330 were found lying on their back and thirty-five were buried face-down, the reasons for which are uncertain. Of the thirty-five, there were fourteen female adults, thirteen male adults, three children and three of uncertain sex and age, and so there is no marked association of these face-down burials with either sex. It has been suggested that they were criminals or had died of contagious disease, but there are no signs of any having suffered a violent death or of any physical abnormalities.

The only evidence from the Bath Gate cemetery which can be used to determine the manner of burial is the presence of coffin nails or fittings. Many graves showed evidence of a wooden coffin, but there was only one case of recognisable coffin fittings, consisting of two iron brackets or hinges. Stone coffins have been recorded in Cirencester since the early nineteenth century, and twenty-five are now known, all from the west of the town close to the source of the limestone from which they were made. Two examples of lead coffins or linings have been noted, one in the nineteenth century and the other during construction work in the 1970s. The latter was found inside a stone coffin which contained the skeleton of a child, as was the case with a similar burial at Gloucester. This cemetery is known to have been in use in the fourth century but may have started slightly earlier, and, judging from the silver coin of Honorius sealed beneath the vertebra of a skeleton, continued to be used well into the fifth century.

Another large cemetery was found on the sand and gravel beds at Barnwood east of Gloucester. Here pre-Roman and Roman burials are recorded, but the bulk of them date from the first two centuries A.D. One hundred inhumations and fifty cremations were noted from an area just to the north of Ermin Street and about 1.2km west-north-west of the Hucclecote villa. This cemetery must have served a settlement close by and is unlikely to be associated with Gloucester 2.5km away.

Other smaller cemeteries are known mainly as a result of modern development in one form or another. When drains were laid on Long Hill, Colethrop, in the parish of Haresfield, several skeletons were discovered associated with Roman pottery and coins. During quarrying on Kineton Hill, Temple Guiting, at least fifteen interments were noted, including inhumations in stone-lined graves, a wooden coffin and cremations. Of particular interest was the discovery that the skull of one inhumation had been placed at the feet and, in another case, at the knees. At Upper Slaughter burials have been found associated with Romano-British pottery, and a lead coffin has been noted west of Beggy Hill Way in the same parish. Another isolated burial in a lead coffin was unearthed during gravel digging in South Cerney in 1941. Stone coffins have been reported at Bitton, Bourton-on-the-Water, Cold Ashton, Dyrham, Kingscote, Lower Slaughter, Tetbury, Upton and Tormarton.

In the Gloucestershire district an increasing number of late Roman farms are being found to have had their own burial grounds, and presumably all farms had a small burial area somewhere, neither too close to the farmhouse nor on good productive land. After a change of ownership, there is no reason to assume that the new owner used the same burial area; in fact he might well prefer a new one. Large cemeteries associated with well-established villas may not be the norm; instead perhaps we should expect a series of quite small ones dotted around the farm.

9
The Fifth Century

The fourth century marked the height of Britain's prosperity under Roman rule; however, during the second half of that century, there were already signs of a deterioration, not only in Britain, but elsewhere in the Empire. In 383 Magnus Maximus lead a revolt in Britain against the central authority, and from then on the situation in the country went from bad to worse. Reductions in the army in the late fourth century meant that by the beginning of the fifth few regular soldiers were left in Britain: by 407 all these were withdrawn, and the burden of defence rested on the shoulders of the local population and any mercenaries they managed to recruit. In A.D. 410 an appeal to Rome by the threatened landowning class was unsuccessful, and the country was left to its own devices with a resulting decline in civilization.

Despite periods of apparent calm and prosperity, various parts of the province were subjected to barbarian raids during the fourth century; indeed some even took place towards the end of the third. These raids occurred on several fronts both from within the province and from overseas: in the north of Britain attacks came from the Picts, while from the north coast of Europe Germanic peoples were reaching Britain by the end of the third century; from the west came groups of Irish who penetrated South Wales and possibly Devon and Cornwall. As the River Severn was a natural route into the heart of Britain, it would have been necessary to police the river and adjacent land. A fort at Cardiff may have been built to combat these Irish raids and Gloucester must surely have played some part in the defence of the province. The presence of the Roman fleet in the Bristol Channel is hinted at by the inscription on one of the late fourth-century mosaics from the temple at Lydney. The inscription, restored and translated, reads:-

> To the God Nodens, Titus Flavius Senilis, officer in charge of the supply-depot of the fleet, laid this pavement out of the money offerings; the work being in charge of Victorinus, interpreter on the Governor's staff.

This period in our history is most difficult to chronicle precisely by the usual archaeological methods, and written accounts are virtually non-existent. The most usual indication that people were living in towns and villas in the fifth century is that alterations to their buildings were still taking place well after the use of coins and datable pottery ceased. However, the Anglo-Saxon Chronicle records that in A.D. 577 Cuthwine and Caewlin fought against the Britons at Dyrham and killed three kings, Conmail, Condidan and Farinmail, and captured three cities, Gloucester, Cirencester and Bath, all of which suggests that sufficient people were still living in those cities to have made a stand against the army of Cuthwine and Caewlin. If the order given for the cities is the same order as their kings, then Conmail must have been the leader in Gloucester and Condidan at Cirencester. The name Conmail, Mr Wacher points out, is of Celtic derivation and might indicate that at this time Gloucester had already passed into the control of Celtic immigrants from Wales or Ireland. The picture that emerges from excavations at Gloucester is of a run-down city in the late fifth and early sixth century, which may have been subject to periodic flooding. During the excavations on the site of the new Market Hall in 1966-7, the excavators noted clear signs of sub-Roman occupation in one of the buildings, and suggested that some of the vacated Roman buildings were reoccupied and were being lived in at the time of the Battle of Dyrham.

The picture from Cirencester is similar, although here there are more examples of structural alterations which can be dated to the early part of the fifth century. Repairs to the Verulamium Gate were carried out at this time, and the sequence deduced from the fourth-century buildings in *insula* XII indicates that they were occupied well into the fifth century. The forum floors showed signs of extensive wear and regular cleaning, leading some to think that it was in use until the middle of the fifth century. Traffic in the town declined, and a new roadside ditch dug beside Ermin Street in *insula* XXIII never collected any silt from the adjacent road. The presence of two unburied human bodies in this ditch indicates that normal town life had ceased, or even that an epidemic had broken out in the town, although this cannot be proved from the skeletal remains.

Further indications of what was happening in the town at this time have come from the amphitheatre where a large timber building was erected in the arena, and the north-east entrance was reduced in size. With the discovery of a few sherds of fifth- or sixth-century grass-tempered pottery, these observations suggest to Mr. Wacher the possiblity that the amphitheatre was turned into a 'fortified retreat' which was easier to defend than a town of ninety-seven hectares with derelict buildings and a 4km length of defensive wall. Attempts to extend organised town life into the fifth century are based on circumstantial evidence, but this nonetheless supports the idea that people were still living in Gloucester and Cirencester, even if the local and national administrative framework had broken down. For some reason the population declined dramatically in the fifth and sixth centuries and by the Battle of Dyrham, A.D. 577, only a handful of people seem to have remained in the towns, taking quite ingenious steps to defend themselves. The reduction in population may have started much earlier, and Dr. R. Reece believes that even by the third century they were no longer recognisable as towns and that by A.D. 350 had gone, a view not generally accepted by many people at present. It may help, however, to explain the major upheaval that was taking place in the countryside during the late third and early fourth centuries, if one postulates a movement of people from the towns into the countryside; the sudden upsurge in the building of villas at this time might reflect an injection of capital from migrating townsfolk.

The evidence for fifth-century life in villas or villages is far from conclusive. How long they remained viable and whether they continued and evolved into the settlements which are so familiar on today's landscape, we do not know. The enigmatic grass-tempered pottery found on an increasing number of settlements has been traditionally dated to the late fifth or even sixth century, and has been taken to indicate a continuation of life there. It has occurred at Barnsley, Frocester, Kingscote, Uley and Cirencester: at Barnsley it was found on the fields around the villa, but not in the vicinity of the building; at Frocester over one hundred sherds have been noted from the villa and courtyard, which along with a fifth-century timber building in the eastern corner of the courtyard point to a considerable amount of activity.

Professor H.P.R. Finberg's analysis of the estate and parish boundaries at Withington points to the boundary being derived from an estate given to a nunnery by King Ethelred in about A.D. 690. As it seems likely that they would have been given an estate in working order, it must, therefore, have been of some antiquity, and may well have been the same estate that was associated with the Roman villa at Withington. It is an interesting idea that such estates could survive intact until the seventh century, but there is no firm archaeological evidence yet to substantiate Professor Finberg's hypothesis, nor, it must be added, to contradict it.

What does stand out amidst all the conjecture and uncertainty, is that in the second half of the fourth century many villas were having a variety of alterations carried out to their buildings, involving in some cases the laying of expensive mosaic floors. Once the administrative organisation both at a national and local level had collapsed and currency had disintegrated, it would have been nearly impossible for these landowners to convert any surplus made on their estates into tangible benefits, and life for the farmer in the fifth and sixth centuries would have become hard and unpredictable. There is no sign of any villa being plundered and set on fire by marauding Saxons; in fact there is little evidence for any Anglo-Saxon activity in the area before the fifth, or even sixth century.

Four to five hundred years of Roman occupation have left some visible signs on the Gloucestershire landscape. The Roman cities of Gloucester and Cirencester were to become significant towns in the Saxon and medieval period, and to this day are among the largest urban centres in the modern county. Some streets in these towns follow the lines of earlier Roman ones, and the remains of a gate can be seen preserved in Gloucester; the town wall and rampart are visible in Cirencester, and also the amphitheatre. In the countryside there may be some link between Roman and later estates, and sweeping across the county are a number of modern roads following a very close alignment to Roman ones, the two classic examples being the Fosse Way and Ermin Street. To some extent the general pattern of settlement today may be not unlike that of the Roman period, with its mixture of towns, villages, hamlets and isolated farms, all served by a major arterial road system and many hundreds of smaller roads and tracks.

Dates of Principal Roman Emperors

A.D.

41-54	Claudius I
54-68	Nero
69-79	Vespasian
79-81	Titus
81-96	Domitian
96-98	Nerva
98-117	Trajan
117-138	Hadrian
138-161	Antonius Pius
161-180	Marcus Aurelius
180-192	Commodus
193-211	Severus
211-217	Caracalla
218-222	Elagabalus
222-235	Severus Alexander
235-238	Maximinius I
238-244	Gordian III
244-249	Philip I
253-260	Valerian I
260-268	Gallienus
268-270	Claudius II and Victorinus
270-275	Aurelian
284-305	Diocletian
286-293	Carausius
293-296	Allectus
306-337	Constantine the Great
337-350	Constans
337-361	Constantius II
350-353	Magnentius
361-363	Julian
364-375	Valentinian
364-378	Valens
367-383	Gratian
375-392	Valentinian II
379-395	Theodosius I
383-408	Arcadius
395-423	Honorius

Some groups of Emperors are often referred to as follows

Vespasian	69-79		Pius	138-161	
Titus	79-81	Flavian	Aurelius	161-180	Antonine
Domitian	81-96		Commodus	180-192	

Severus	193-211	
Caracalla	211-217	Severan
Elagabalus	218-222	
Severus Alexander	222-235	

Museums and Roman Monuments

Museums with Collections of Roman Material from Gloucestershire

Opening hours vary from one museum to another and sometimes alter during the year. For details visitors are advised to check by telephone.

Chedworth Villa site museum	(Withington 256)
Cheltenham Art Gallery and Museum Service	(Cheltenham 37431)
Corinium Museum, Cirencester	(Cirencester 5611)
Gloucester City Museum and Art Gallery	(Gloucester 24131)
Lydney Park Site Museum	(Dean 42844)
Stroud and District Museum	(Stroud 3394)
Sudeley Castle	(Winchcombe 602308)

There is also some Gloucestershire material in the Ashmolean Museum, Oxford, Birmingham City Museum, The British Museum and Bristol City Museum.

Roman Remains to be seen in Gloucestershire

Only those which are open to the public are listed

Chedworth Roman Villa	- National Trust.
Cirencester	- Amphitheatre - entrance from Cotswold Ave.
	Town Wall - entrance from Abbey Grounds or Corinium Gate.
Gloucester	- Town wall visible in Museum basement.
	- East Gate – beneath Boots store.

Great Witcombe Roman Villa   - Closed to the public at the time of writing.

Lydney Roman temple and iron mine - Limited opening. Parties by arrangement.

A stretch of Roman road is visible at Blackpool Bridge in the Forest of Dean (National Grid Reference SO 6508). For further details of all sites, see R.J.A. Wilson, *A Guide to the Roman Remains in Britain*.

Excavations take place in the county from time to time and details can be obtained from museums.

A reconstruction of the Woodchester Orpheus mosaic pavement can be seen at the Rev Rowland Hill's Tabernacle Church, Wotton-under-Edge (Wotton-under-Edge 3380)

Bibliography

The Royal Commission On Historical Monuments *Inventory of Iron Age and Romano-British Monuments in the Gloucestershire Cotswolds* (H.M.S.O. 1976) is the most detailed survey of Roman sites in the Cotswolds and contains many references.

Two annual publications report on recent finds and contain more detailed articles on specific topics:-
a *Transactions of the Bristol and Gloucestershire Archaeological Society*
b *Glevensis* - The review of the Gloucester and District Archaeological Research Group.

Bathurst, W.H.,	*Roman Antiquities at Lydney Part, Glos.* London. 1879
Branigan, K.	'Gauls in Gloucestershire?'. *TBGAS* 92(1973), 82-95
Branigan, K.	*The Roman Villa in South-West England.* Bradford on Avon. 1977
Brown, P.D.C. & McWhirr, A.D.	'Cirencester, 1966'. *Antiquaries Journal* 47(1967), 185-197
Clifford, E.M.	'The Roman Villa, Hucclecote near Gloucester'. *TBGAS* 55(1933), 323-373
Clifford, E.M.	'Roman Altars in Gloucestershire'. *TBGAS* 60(1938) 297-307
Eagles, B.N. & Swan, V.G.	'The Chessalls, a Romano-British Settlement at Kingscote'. *TBGAS* 91(1972), 60-91
Ellison, A.	*Excavations at West Hill Uley 1977-9.* British Archaeological Reports No. 77 Oxford. 1980. Pages 305-328
Finberg, H.P.R.	*Roman and Saxon Withington.* Occasional paper No 8 Department of English Local History, University of Leicester, 1955
Fowler, P.J.	'Archaeology and the M5 Motorway, Gloucestershire 1969-75; a summary and assessment. *TBGAS* 95(1977), 40-6
Fullbrook-Leggatt, L.E.W.O.	*Roman Gloucester.* Gloucester. 1968
Gascoigne, P.E.	'Clear Cupboard Villa, Farmington'. *TBGAS* 88(1969), 34-67
Gracie, H.S.	'Frocester Court Roman Villa; First Report'. *TBGAS* 89(1970), 15-86.
Gracie, H.S. & Price, E.G.	'Frocester Court Roman Villa; Second Report' *TBGAS* 97(1980), 9-64

Goodburn, R.	*The Roman Villa, Chedworth*. London. 1972
Hart, C.	*Archaeology in Dean*. Gloucester. 1967
Hassall, M. & Rhodes, J.	'Excavations at the New Market Hall, Gloucester'. *TBGAS* 93(1974), 15-100
Heighway, C.	*Ancient Gloucester*. Gloucester. 1976
Heighway, C. *et al*	'Excavations at Gloucester. Fourth Interim Report: St Oswald's Priory, Gloucester, 1975-6' *Antiquaries Journal* 58(1978).103-132
Heighway, C.	*Excavation of the North and East Gates of Gloucester, 1974*. Forthcoming
Hunter, A.G.	'A Romano-British Bath Block at Trevor Road, Hucclecote, Glos' *TBGAS* 79(1960), 159-173
Hurst, H.	'Excavations at Gloucester, 1968-1971: First Interim Report' *Antiquaries Journal* 52(1972), 24-69
Hurst, H.	'Excavations at Gloucester, 1971-1973: Second Interim Report' *Antiquaries Journal* 54(1974), 8-52
Hurst, H. *et al*	'Excavations at Gloucester: Third Interim Report: Kingsholm 1966-1975' *Antiquaries Journal* 55(1975), 267-294
Hurst, H.	'Gloucester (Glevum): A Colonia in the West Country' in Branigan, K. & Fowler, P.J. *The Roman West Country*. Newton Abbot. 1976
McWhirr, A.D.	'Cirencester (Corinium): A Civitas Capital in the West Country' in Branigan, K. and Fowler, P.J., 1976
McWhirr, A.D. (Ed)	*Studies in the Archaeology and History of Cirencester*. Oxford. 1976
McWhirr, A.D.	'Cirencester' in *Current Archaeology* 29 Nov 1971, 144-52 & 42, Jan 1974 216-9
McWhirr, A.D.	'Cirencester 1969-72: Ninth Interim Report' *Antiquaries Journal* 53(1973), 191-218
McWhirr, A.D.	'Cirencester 1973-6: Tenth Interim Report' *Antiquaries Journal* 58(1978), 61-80
McWhirr, A.D. & Viner, D.	Region' *Britannia* 9(1978), 359-377 'The Production and Distribution of Tiles in Roman Britain with particular reference to Cirencester Region'
McWhirr, A.D. & Wacher, J.S.	*Cirencester Excavations Vol 1: Early Military History*. Forthcoming
Neal, D.S.	'Witcombe Roman Villa: A Reconstruction' in Apted, M.R., Gilyard-Beer, R. and Saunders, A.D. (Eds) *Ancient Monuments and their Interpretation*. Chichester 1977

O'Neil, H.E.   'The Roman Settlement on the Fosse Way at Bourton Bridge, Bourton-on-the-Water, Glos'. *TBGAS* 87(1968), 29-55

Oswald, A.   'Roman Material from Dorn, Gloucestershire' *TBGAS* 82(1964), 18-24

Rhodes, J.F.   *Roman-Britjsh Sculptures in the Gloucester City Museum*. Gloucester. 1964

Richmond, I.A.   'The Four Coloniae of Roman Britain'. *Archaeological Journal* 103(1946) 57-84

Scott Garrett, C.   'Chesters Roman Villa, Woolaston, Glos' *Archaeologia Cambrensis* 93(1938), 93,-125

Swain, E.J.   *Excavations The Chessalls, Kingscote*. Interim reports 1975-9

Wacher, J.S.   'Cirencester 1960: First Interim Report' *Antiquaries Journal* 41(1961), 63-71

Wacher, J.S.   'Cirencester 1961: Second Interim Report' *Antiquaries Journal* 42(1962), 1-14

Wacher, J.S.   'Cirencester 1961: Second Interim Report' *Antiquaries Journal* 42(1962), 1-14

Wacher, J.S.   'Cirencester 1962: Third Interim Report' *Antiquaries Journal* 43(1963), 15-26

Wacher, J.S.   'Cirencester 1963: Fourth Interim Report' *Antiquaries Journal* 44(1964), 9-18

Wacher, J.S.   'Cirencester 1964: Fifth Interim Report' *Antiquaries Journal* 45(1965), 97-110

Webster, G.A.   'Cirencester, Dyer Court Excavations 1957' *TBGAS* 78(1959), 44-85.

Zeepvat, R.J.   'Observations in Dyer Street and Market Place, Cirencester' *TBGAS*, 97(1980), 65-73

For some general books on Roman Britain see:-

Frere, S.S.   *Britannia*. London 1967 and later editions

Rivet, A.L.F.   *Town and Country in Roman Britain* London 1964

Scullard, H.H.   *Roman Britain — Outpost of the Empire*. London 1979

Wacher, J.S.   *Roman Britain*. London 1978 and *Towns of Roman Britain*. London 1975

Acknowledgements

Many people have helped in the preparation of this book, some by providing illustrations and others by discussing problems with the author. The Royal Commission on Historical Monuments has generously allowed plans from their *Inventory of Iron Age and Romano-British Monuments in the Gloucestershire Cotswolds* to be used, and the Secretary of the Commission, Dr P.J. Fowler, has been of the greatest assistance throughout the preparation of the book.

All the museums and archaeological units in the county have been most willing to provide figures and plates, and these are acknowledged below. Many individuals have made the task of writing this book less onerous and even a pleasure; they include Dr Ann Ellison, R. Goodburn, Carolyn Heighway. Dr. N. Herbert, H. Hurst, P. Leach, Dr. R. Leech, D.S. Neal, E.G. Price, Mary Parris, J.F. Rhodes, Janet Richardson, E.G. Swain, D.J. Viner, Linda Viner, M.J. Watkins, Dr. G.A. Webster, and D.R. Wilson.

Helen McWhirr spent many hours assisting with editorial matters and David Viner has kindly read through the text making valuable points to ponder over.

The author gratefully acknowledges the following for permission to use illustrative material:

Bath Museum 140
British Museum 108, 126, 127, 144, 145
The Cambridge University Committee for Aerial Photography Frontispiece, 131, 159
The Cirencester Excavation Committee 4, 9, 10, 29, 31, 33, 34, 35, 36, 37, 39, 46, 48, 50, 51, 53, 54, 55, 56, 57, 146, 148
Corinium Museum 6, 8, 32, 53, 106, 115, 121, 122, 138, 142, 160, 161
Committee for Rescue Archaeology in Avon, Gloucestershire and Somerset 157
Ermin Street Guard 20, and front cover illustration.
Gloucester City Museum 13, 127
Gloucester City Excavation Unit 12, 15, 16, 17, 18, 24, 25, 26, 27, 41, 42, 43, 44, 45
Kingscote Archaeological Association 75, 76
Marley Photography 13
Neal, D.S. 92, 93
Middleton, 87
Pennycuick, D. Dr. 76

The figures contained in this book have been drawn by a variety of people and in particular Richard Bryant has been responsible for many of the plans of Gloucester and Nick Griffiths has redrawn several plans and drawn the reconstruction on page 40. The photographs of recent excavations and objects from Cirencester have been taken by a number of people including W.J. Barrett, C.J. Bowler, R. Pears and C.J. Shuttleworth.

Index

Illustrations are shown separately in bold type at the end of each entry